BEYOND RELIGION

INDESCRIBABLE

The Adventures of A. Soul

Volume 4

W. A. VEGA

Global Publishing Group LLC

Scripture references are generally taken from the New King James and the Complete Jewish Study Bible Version.

Printed in the United States of America

First trade edition

ISBN 978-1-7212135-0-4

*"Your eyes saw my substance, being yet
unformed. And in Your book, they all were
written, the days fashioned for me, when as yet
there were none of them.*

*How precious also are Your thoughts to me, O God!
How great is the sum of them!"*

(Psalm 139: 16-17)

DEDICATION

To My Beloved Bride

"My love to you," says the Bridegroom, "is indescribable. It far exceeds the love of ten-thousand lovers; more intense than the energy of the sun at noonday; altogether greater than all the stars above and all the grains of sand on the earth beneath. If every ocean, river, lake, and stream in all the world were emptied and each drop of water counted, its measure would pale in comparison to the greatness of my love for you. It overflows with greater intensity than infinite erupting volcanoes. 'You have ravished my heart...' *(Song of Solomon 4: 9)* Death cannot contain it and eternity isn't long enough to experience it. All the definitions and expressions of love in every language, culture, tribe, tongue and nation cannot adequately describe it. I designed it that way, my Beloved, my Bride, for my love is beyond human comprehension."

"Your love," responds the Bride, "my Beloved, my Bridegroom, makes me breathless, at the mention of your name. Yes, I am my Beloved's and His desire is toward me." *(Song of Solomon 7:10)*

I thank my Lord, my God, who gave the mandate to:

"Write the vision

And make it plain on tablets,

That he may run who reads it.

For the vision is yet for an appointed time;

But at the end it will speak, and it will not lie.

Though it tarries, wait for it;

Because it will surely come,

It will not tarry.

Behold the proud,

His soul is not upright in him;

But the just shall live by his faith."

(Habakkuk 2: 2 – 4)

PREFACE

In the infinite realm of NOW there lived a Father, His only Son and their Spirit, named Breath. The three were inseparable.

At some point in NOW, the Father, His Son and Breath had a special meeting. Before the meeting began, the Son eagerly said, "Father, I know what this is all about. It's what we've been planning, isn't it? I've been fervently waiting for your Word."

The Father replied, "Son, you know everything about me. Do you know why I delayed this meeting?"

"Yes, Father," the son answered solemnly. "We've never been separated and this could require us to be separated. I know how difficult this will be, but I'm ready. I want what you want more than anything, regardless the cost. It's what we've always wanted."

Breath, who was unusually still, chimed in excitedly, "Just say the Word, and it's done."

The Father pensively paused and said, "Okay, I know we're in one accord. Son, I'm ready to give you a bride."

"And I'm ready to give you many sons and daughters to enjoy the love we share," replied the Son with exuberant delight. "I'm ready Abba."

Bouncing with excitement, and ready for action, Breath exclaimed, "Just say the Word, and it's done."

Knowing the magnitude of what was ahead, the Father asked, "Are you sure Son? It will cost us everything."

"Yes," the Son answered. "But because this is our desire, the cost will be pure joy. Breath is always with me, and I know You are to. Our plan has always been to expand our Kingdom and share our love. I want what you want more than anything. I'm ready, Father."

Gazing adoringly into His son's eyes, his Father pulled him closer. Their love was indescribable. The Father knew His Son would do anything for Him and the Son was fully assured that His father would do the same. Their hearts were intertwined in thought, word and deed. For as long as they existed, they had always been one, sharing one Spirit. The Son was confident that there was absolutely nothing that could separate Him from His father's love, and likewise, the Father knew His son's heart of unconditional love.

Consequently, the Son, not having seen his bride, was already in love, and looked forward to the day when He would present His Father with many sons and daughters.

With their pure, undefiled, indescribable, immeasurable love exploding into new life, Breath leapt into action. The Word was spoken and in six days a new realm was created. Breath was released and a new dominion of time, space, matter, and life burst into creation. On the sixth day, the Father proudly presented his Son with His bride. Zealous to please the Father, the Son was enthralled with the prospect of adding many children to their Kingdom. All made in their image and likeness, with One Spirit, sharing their indescribable love.

With the fullness of Breath infusing life into lifeless forms, this Bride had the ability to choose. However, there was only one choice the Father longed for them to choose ~ His son. Likewise, there was only one choice the Son longed for them to choose, His Father. And Breath hoovered over them, ready to spring into action, leading them to choose both the Father and His Son.

Whatever their choice, they were ready with a plan to win the Brides' affection, even unto death and separation, and be forever joined in union with them, in the realm of NOW.

INTRODUCTION
THE DREAM – PART ONE

"You wouldn't believe the dream I had last night," exclaimed A. Soul. "It was as if I went on a long trip into another reality."

"Really," replied Joy Grace in an affirming, yet unsurprised, tone. "Please share, I can't wait to hear it."

Without hesitation, A. Soul began to describe her reality like dream, pausing occasionally for breath.

"It began when I felt a Breath, as if whispered in my inner ear, inviting me to 'Come up here.' The Breath sounded, felt, smelled and tasted as smooth as melted butter on freshly baked bread and as soft as a chocolate soufflé. I couldn't resist so sweet and gentle an invitation. So, I answered, 'Yes,' turned around and went back to sleep."

She paused for a moment and then continued, "No sooner had I fallen asleep when I was fully awake again. This time, I was standing in the middle of a large open space. It felt like an enclosed garden, the size of a hundred football fields. I inhaled incredible floral fragrances that wafted in and out in sparkling, gentle waves. The floor was marble like silk, warm, soft and soothing to the feet. A rainbow of colors glistened in playful delight above and within the space. Everything around me felt as if teeming with exuberant life energy, yet there was no evidence of life as far as my eyes could see.

Drinking in the breathtaking atmosphere, I finally found my voice and asked in awe, 'Where is this place? What is this place?'

As I looked around in stunned amazement, I saw that I was surrounded by shelves of books as far as my eyes could see. There was a large section of blue and pink covered books directly in front of me. To the right, there was another section of red and white covered books. To the left, I saw purple, yellow, orange and brown books. Within and around light from above bounced off the colorful books and created a surreal, kaleidoscope effect.

There appeared to be millions of green books on tables, some opened and some closed. Every shade of green was visible, from the brightest to the darkest. Looking closer, many green books appeared darker as grey and black hues hovered over them. By contrast, the brighter green books flickered with luminous, translucent, jeweled colored radiant light, as if glowing from within. There was continuous movement among the opened and closed green books, as if an invisible hand weaved in and through them.

I walked around in silent wonder and caught my breath when I heard soft music emanating as if from the books themselves. Glancing at an open book, I reached out and barely touched it, when a delicious wave of electricity surged through my body. I jumped away and declared, 'It's as if this book is alive.'

The Breath said in a musical tone of a gentle waterfall, 'They are all alive. Even though you see unlimited books, they are all really one book. We call it the Book of Life. Each book contains the life and story of everyone who has life today, including the pre-born, the unborn, those who are alive today yet dead; and those who are dead yet alive. Each contains two parallel stories, the plan and purpose we designed from the foundation of the world; and the plan the Father's sons and daughters choose for themselves. We celebrate when both stories eventually merge.'

Gazing in awe, with myriads of questions invading my mind simultaneously, I finally spoke again and asked, 'Is my story in one of these books?'

'Of course,' answered the mesmerizing Breath now emanating sparkles of iridescent light. Pointing to a set of green books that were closed, the Breath came closer and whispered intimately in my ear, 'Yes, your story is in one of these books.'

My heart leapt with unbridled excitement mingled with a hint of apprehension. I asked, 'But why is it closed?'

The Breath, in loving, paternal tones as if emanating from a field of dandelions dancing in the wind, answered and said, 'It's closed because your story is sealed. No one can change it but you, but we know that you want what we want, more than anything. You are forever sealed in the Father's plan. *(Jeremiah 29:11)* This means that all things are working together for good, and that includes everything; the good, the bad, and the ugly, because we know you love us. *(Romans 8:28)* You are secure in us and we are in you, just like the Son is in the Father and the Father is in the Son.' *(John 15)*

Digressing from sharing her dream, A. Soul said in utter amazement, "Joy Grace, this was the most remarkable dream I've ever had, and there's more. As the Breath spoke, I felt wave upon wave of velvet like breezes cover my entire body. It's as if I had jumped into a pool of warm, chocolate ice cream and floated on a mound of vanilla whipped cream. Words cannot describe the experience."

She smiled and then continued, "I felt as if I was the most important person in the world as I stood in this presence. I felt bold and confidently began asking other questions. The truth, Joy Grace, is that I didn't want this experience to end.

"What questions did you ask?" Joy Grace replied.

"Why are most of the green books opened?" I asked.

'Very observant, A. Soul,' answered the affirming Breath. 'Remember, this is the Book of Life. Therefore, everyone who is alive today on earth are written in the green books, the born again, and those yet to be born again. You see, fullness of life is given at the time of heavenly conception, at the foundation of the world. *(Psalm 139:15-16)*

For God so loved the world, that He gave His only begotten Son so that whosoever, believes in Him shall not perish but have everlasting life. *(John 3:16)*

'God gave His Son, as Redeemer, Savior, Deliverer, to all; the good, the bad, and the ugly, at the beginning of their heavenly conception. His heart is that none would perish. He doesn't want to be separated from any of His children.'

The Breath paused and with a hint of delightful melodies springing as if from a harp, said, 'We call Him the eternal optimist as He's always believing and pursuing His sons and daughters even up to their last breath. His one desire is that they accept the gift of His son's life, in exchange for their eternal separation from Him.'

The Breath began drifting upward in subdued tones of grey, purple, pinks and blues, and shared solemnly, 'If every life we conceived could only understand how much your heavenly Father loves you. He never, ever wants to be separated from you, just as He never wanted to be separated from His Son. And He's felt that way the moment He first conceived of you from the foundation of the world. *(Psalm 139:15-16)* Yes, even before your mother knew of your conception, you and every life belonged to Him and He doesn't want to lose not one.'

Again, digressing from relating her dream, A. Soul said, "Joy Grace, it was then that tears began rolling down my face as the thought of the Father's indescribable love left me speechless."

INTRODUCTION – PART TWO
THE DREAM CONTINUED

"Joy Grace," continued A. Soul, "I'm not sure how long I was silent, but it seemed like an eternity. I have heard John 3:16 all my life, and thought I understood this love. What the Breath shared was, and still is, overwhelming. Just as the verse reads, 'Such knowledge is too wonderful for me; it is high, I cannot attain it.' *(Psalm 139:6).* I knew this was beyond my limited human capacity."

"I know what you mean," added Joy Grace. "Their love for the world is as indescribable as their love for each other. Since you had the dream, do you believe you better understand this love?"

"I do, but don't believe it is humanly possible to fully comprehend it. This love is unfathomable. How can one describe the grandeur and magnitude of the sky or the limitlessness of the ocean without ever seeing it?

Or how can one describe the designs and colors on the wings of butterflies? The most amazing thing though, is that while I can't adequately comprehend this incredible love, I am experiencing it, since I joyfully accepted the love of the Father's gift of His Son, Jesus Christ."

She continued in awe, "Now I know that this incredible, indescribable love was mine from the foundation of the world. Before my mother and father conceived me, regardless of how my conception on earth took place, I was marinated in their love. I was wrapped in it and born with the knowledge of it in the deepest part of my inner being. It's what my heart yearns and searches for all my life."

With tears brimming in her eyes, A. Soul whispered, "Joy Grace, you know my story here on earth. This love eluded me for some time. I knew that I was made to be loved and to love. Now it's so clear to me. The day I opened my heart and accepted this gift of love, I received the fullness of the love between the Father, the Son and their Spirit. But it has taken me over thirty-years to believe it and embrace its fullness, when it was mine all along. This knowledge is so tremendous, who can contain it?"

Fully understanding the significance of this moment for A. Soul, Joy Grace, reached over and embraced her dear friend. They hugged, as A. Soul, heaved with tears flowing freely. When she began to be quieted, Joy Grace added, "Yes, this love is incredible and everyone who has breath on earth now, has the same access to it as you do. The Father gave the same gift to the world, to whosoever will, regardless of past, present or future. This gift of love is available, but must be fully accepted, just as you did. This is good news A. Soul, why the tears?"

"I know that not every name is in the Book of Life as many die without accepting the gift of His Son," replied A. Soul.

"Yes, this is sad, but true," responded Joy Grace. "But remember, God gives us a gift, and it's our choice to accept or reject it. Love can never be forced. So, from heaven's perspective, those who willfully choose to decline this gift, receive what they wanted, separation from Him. While their rejection grieves the Father's heart,

He accepts it, and so must we. What you experienced in your dream was a celebration of life, everlasting life. The Father with His sons and daughters, and the Son with His Bride. This is a fulfillment of their vision from before the foundation of the world."

"It's even clearer to me now," said A. Soul. "This has never been about religion. It's always been about being part of an amazing love relationship between the Father and His Son."

"It always has and always will be," replied Joy Grace. "God wants sons and daughters as a Bride for His Son. He's not interested in religious or robotic followers. It began out of love and will, for eternity, always be about love. It's a contagious love that must be shared with others because it's beyond human capacity to contain."

"Amazing," repeated A. Soul who was still at a loss for words as she sat gazing into the distance. "But there's more of the dream to share. It gets even more incredible."

INTRODUCTION – PART 3
THE DREAM – CONCLUSION

Continuing to share her dream, A. Soul said, "The blue books caught my attention, so I asked, 'Whose stories are in the blue books?'

The Breath, as if already knowing my questions, answered with the sound of tinkling wind chimes swaying gleefully in the gentle breeze, 'Those are the stories of the unborn baby boys, and you've probably already guessed, the pink books are the stories of unborn baby girls.'

I asked, 'How can the unborn have stories, since they never experienced life?'

'From heaven's perspective, they have life,' replied the Breath in warm shades of pinks and blues. *(Psalm 139:15-16)* 'In fact, they are the ones who have known perfect life. Just because they were never born on earth, doesn't mean that they are not alive. The unborn have never tasted death. Remember, real death is eternal separation from the Father. They have always been alive and their stories are perfectly preserved here. We especially love reading their stories.'

'This is tremendous, I would love to hear some of their stories,' I said, gazing upward in wonder. Then I asked, 'What are in the red books?'

The Breath paused before answering as hues of gold, reds, pinks, browns, and oranges filled the atmosphere. An intoxicating aroma of exotic spices warmed the senses with each sound. The tone was thick with humility and pregnant with pride, 'You asked about the red books. They contain the names and stories of those martyred for accepting the gift. All the names and stories contained in these books are fascinating. Stories that appear incomplete, wasted or insignificant on earth are completed and significant in heaven. *(Matthew 5:2-12)* The least on earth is the greatest in heaven, and the weakest and most defenseless on earth is the strongest in heaven.'

'Can I read some of these stories?' I asked.

'These books are not to be to read,' answered the Breath as jewel like tones of sapphire, ruby, diamonds, and emeralds gracefully swirled around before drifting upward. 'Remember, they are living stories. They are to be experienced. They are to be felt. They are to be known.'

Clearly not understanding what I had just heard, I squinted my eyes and furrowed my brows. Noticing my questioning look, the Breath released sparks of silver before answering, 'Let me show you what I mean.'

In an instant, four books with different colors appeared before me. They were glistening in rainbow like colors. I was mesmerized. Then noticing there were no green books, I curiously asked, 'There are no green books here?'

'No one has access to the green books,' said the Breath, 'but the Father and whomever He grants permission to encounter that life. Not even the host of heaven is allowed access to those. They are vigilantly guarded.'

'So what stories can I experience?' I asked.

Illuminated in radiant light, with hints of green, purple, yellow and blue arising in a delightful aroma of daisies, lilies and daffodils,

the Breath answered, 'You can choose from any of
the books in front of you. The stories are familiar
but I know you'll be surprised with heaven's
perspective of each one.'

The Breath then slowly drifted upwards
leaving tiny, sparks of twinkling earth hues as He
ascended. Sadly, I knew the conversation had
ended.

Then pausing in reverent silence at the
prospect of opening one of the books, I
contemplated which to open first. And opening
the first page of one, I was mysteriously
transported into the story. I remember each
vividly, because I not only read them, I
experienced them. Then I awoke to find that I
was back in bed."

"I can't wait to hear the stories you read in
the Book," said Joy Grace as her eyes twinkled in
fiery shades of silver and flashing sparks of gold.
"I've been waiting for the day when you would
experience the stories from heaven's perspective.
It's when your perspectives change that you see
what I see, and it's all good. As God works all
things together for good to those who love Him,

who are called and chosen, for His purposes."
(Romans 8:28)

A. Soul caught her breath in bewilderment when she saw her friend and companion's eyes sparkle with delight. With her heart overflowing with excitement and her voice increasing to another octave, she said, "Joy Grace, it's as if I was watching a movie, as each story unfolded before my eyes. They all had a common theme, in that they all began with conception from the foundation of the world. And the most amazing of all, was that there were no endings." *(Psalm 139:15-16)*

Then with the details of camera lenses, A. Soul related several snippets of a continuous story of one man's descendants. Each one, a living, open book, written in the Book of Life, all with a common theme.

May these fictional perspectives of biblical realities, bless you as they captivated A. Soul, on the night she answered, "Yes," to the Breath that invited her to "Come up here."

"But you are a chosen generation, a royal priesthood, a holy nation, His own special people, that you may proclaim the praises of Him who called you out of darkness into His marvelous light."

(1Peter 2:9)

BOOK ONE

THE FIRST DAUGHTER OF JACOB

Sometime between1836 BC – 1689 BC

Somewhere in Paddan Aram, Mesopotamia (parts of modern day Iraq/Syria/Turkey)

CHAPTER 1
CURIOSITY

"No one understands me," she whimpered and then continued. "Mother, you don't know what it's like being the only daughter amongst twelve brothers. I love them, but they don't understand me. They treat me like one of the boys and I'm not. Mother, please, let me go into this village and visit the land. Who knows, I might meet other girls my age and we can become friends."

Nodding with understanding, her mother replied, "I do understand daughter, but you cannot go wondering into this strange village alone. I'm sure one of your brothers would be happy to go with you."

"No mother. That won't work, because if other young women are there, they won't approach me when they see me with a boy, even if it is my brother. I have to go alone," the young lady stubbornly insisted.

Replying in a sterner, more authoritative tone, her mother replied, "No, and that's final. No further argument. I know you're bold and adventurous, but I will not permit you to go into this unknown village alone. If you go, you will have to take at least one of your brothers with you. I'm sure they will be delighted to be your escort."

Shrugging her shoulders, she retorted, "Okay, if you insist, I'll go with one of my brothers, but I *am* going."

Her mother commented, "God, why are all my children so strong-willed and headstrong?"

Sixteen-year-old Dinah grinned, reached out and kissed her, then said, "Thanks mother, you are the best. I love you so much and I will be careful. There's nothing to worry about."

Running into the first brother she saw, she asked, "Joseph, will you come with me to visit this village?"

He replied, "Not now, Dinah, father and I are doing inventory, but perhaps tomorrow. Why do you want to visit this village anyway? You know most villagers are suspicious of us."

"Yes, I know, you've all told me that a thousand times," Dinah answered. "But I want to meet the other girls here and see what their life is like. I'm just curious, that's all. They are probably just as eager to know about us as well."

"Unfortunately, not today Dinah. In fact, we're all helping father with inventory," Joseph replied.

Dinah's shoulders drooped as she said, "Perhaps tomorrow then, but I know we usually leave shortly after inventory, so I may not get to visit them at all. Thanks anyway."

Joseph returned to his task, while Dinah gazed longingly in the direction of the nearby village. Then, overcome with interest, she began walking in the direction of her gaze. The further she walked, the stronger her interest grew, until she found herself within a few yards of the city gate. She thought to herself, *Well, I've already come this far, I might as well go in to see the daughters of the land. (Genesis 34:1)* And, with a few more steps, she entered the village.

CHAPTER 2

DISHONOR

Like her grandmother, Rebekah, and her aunt Rachel, Dinah was a stunning beauty. She was taller than the average woman of her time, with jet, black hair that tumbled to her waist. Her piercing, black, almond shaped eyes compelled attention and were perfectly set in a heart shaped face. High cheekbones framed a perfectly sculpted nose that sat above exquisitely contoured lips.

Although fully covered in traditional attire of the day, the outline of her figure was lovely in form and shape. Her countenance, however, was her most attractive feature. Her face and eyes shined with kindness, compassion, and friendliness. She knew no strangers and felt comfortable in any setting.

Being the only girl among twelve brothers, she was especially at ease with boys. Therefore, it was not surprising when she was approached by three young men, that she bowed in acknowledgement and continued moving forward. Speaking to his companions, Shechem, the prince of the village, asked incredulously, "Who is _that_? She is the most beautiful girl I've ever seen. I haven't seen her here before."

"I haven't seen her either," one of his companions answered. "She must be visiting from the group that's camped outside our village. I wonder if they sent her to spy on us?"

"She's too pretty to be a spy, but I'll find out," Shechem replied.

Leaving his friends, he turned in the direction Dinah walked and began following. Finally, within speaking range, he said, "My name is Shechem. I'm the prince of this land, my father Hamor is the leader. I don't believe I've seen you here before. Where are you visiting from?"

Knowing no strangers, Dinah bowed and said, "My name is Dinah. I am with my father, Jacob's household, and just wanted to visit your village."

Shechem said, "I would love to show you around. We're a small group, but have settled here for some time. This is my home, my father calls it Shechem, after his father and grandfather; and it's also my name."

Dinah, who viewed Shechem as she did one of her brothers, replied, "Thanks, I would like that. I especially want to meet other girls in your village."

Shechem replied, "I know the perfect place to begin. Let's start with my father's house as my sisters and their friends will be there."

Excited at the prospect of meeting girls her age, she said, "Thanks, I'm looking forward to meeting them."

Amazed at her courage and independence, he instructed, "Follow me. The pleasure will be all mine."

Within minutes, they entered his father's house. Unaware, Dinah followed him to his private quarters where he assaulted her. Many heard her screams and pleas for help, but no one came to her rescue.

CHAPTER 3

INDULGENCE

Hurt, devastated, afraid and ashamed by her experience, Dinah sat crumbled on the floor. Immediately regretting his impulsive behavior, Shechem confessed his love and desire to have her as his wife. Reaching to console Dinah, he said, "I must have you as a wife. I will do anything to have you. My father will talk to your father and get it all arranged."

Shrinking from his touch, Dinah pulled her outer garment closer to her chest and did not respond. With her mind racing, all she thought of were her mother's last words.

With tears streaming down her cheeks, she said, "I can't go home now and I don't know where to go."

Attempting to reassure her, Shechem said, "You can stay with us. I want you to stay with us. Don't be afraid, my father will take care of everything. You will be my wife."

Dinah didn't respond.

Without another word, Shechem went to his father's quarters and shared what he had done. His father, who indulged his son, reassured him that everything would be okay. "I'm sure we will be able to work things out between them and us. We're a larger company of people and I'm sure her father would make an alliance between us. Let's go to them and present our proposition."

Shechem hugged him and said, "You always have the answers, father, thank you. You will love her. She is beautiful, friendly and kind. I can't live without her even though we just met. You must get me this young woman as a wife."

Then Hamor [his father] went out to Jacob to speak with him. And the sons of Jacob came in from the field when they heard it, and the men were grieved and very angry, because he had done a disgraceful thing in Israel by lying with Jacob's daughter, a thing which ought not to be done.

But Hamor spoke with them, saying, "The soul of my son Shechem longs for your daughter.

Please give her to him as a wife. And make marriages with us; give your daughters to us, and take our daughters to yourselves. So you shall dwell with us, and the land shall be before you. Dwell and trade in it, acquire possessions for yourselves in it."

Then Shechem said to her father and her brothers, "Let me find favor in your eyes and whatever you say to me I will give. Ask me ever so much dowry and gift, and I will give according to what you say to me, but give me the young woman as a wife."

But the sons of Jacob answered Shechem and Hamor, his father, and spoke deceitfully, because he had defiled Dinah their sister. And they said to them, "We cannot do this thing, to give our sister to one who is uncircumcised, for that would be a reproach to us. But on this *condition,* we will consent to you: If you will become as we are, if every male of you is circumcised, then we will give our daughters to you, and we will take your daughters to us; and we will dwell with you, and we will become one people. But if you will not heed us and be circumcised, then we will take our daughter and be done."

And their words pleased Hamor and Shechem. So, the young man did not delay to do the things because he delighted in Jacob's daughter. *(Genesis 34:6-18)*

The following day, Hamor, Shechem and all the males in their city were circumcised.

CHAPTER 4
STRATEGY

"We must strike quickly and suddenly. They're weak and defenseless right now." Simeon whispered to his brother.

"I think we need to let our other brothers and father know what we're about to do," replied Levi.

"Absolutely not. We don't have time to debate if we should proceed. How dare these uncircumcised savages think they could get away with what they did. The audacity of them thinking that we will ever be one with them. They obviously don't know who they are dealing with," Simeon retorted. "This will be quick and easy. They won't even know what hit them."

Being less impetuous, Levi responded hesitantly, "Okay, I agree, but..."

Cutting him off mid-sentence, Simeon declared, "There's no but...we need to do it and do it now. Everyone is guilty and they will pay.

We also need to send a strong message that we will not be taken advantage of by any of the cities we pass through."

"I know you're right but I also know there will be consequences," Levi conceded. "Okay, let's do it."

Hastily planning their strategy, they inconspicuously strolled into the city later that day. Levi went to Shechem's private quarters, while Simeon waited nearby for his signal. Seeing someone he believed to be a servant, Levi said, "I'm Dinah's brother. I want to see Shechem."

The woman led him to Shechem who was lying in bed, feverish with pain. Upon seeing him, Shechem grimaced and said, "Forgive me for not getting up, but I'm in pain. This is the most painful experience I've ever had. I hope you know I'm sincere in what I shared. I love your sister and will do anything to have her as a wife."

Levi nodded in agreement and said, "We look forward to having you in the family. Where's Dinah. I have something for her."

"She's in the next room," Shechem answered. "I know she's still adjusting to being here, but you'll see, she will grow to love us as we love her."

Levi gave him a half smile and responded, "Great, I'll stroll over to find her. Hope you recover soon. By the way, our agreement was that every male would undergo circumcision, right?"

Shechem nodded and said, "Yes, this is the third day since our circumcision. I imagine everyone is just as weak from pain as I am. We gave you our word."

Leaving the room, Levi responded, "And we honor your word. Hope you recover soon."

Finding Simeon impatiently pacing outside, they both went to where Dinah was being held. Seeing her sitting between what appeared to be two female servants, Levi said, "We're Dinah's brothers and want to talk to her."

The servants stepped out to allow Dinah to speak with her brothers. Simeon asked, "Are you alright? We heard what happened and we're here to bring you home."

With tears welling up in her eyes, she said, "I've been so afraid. Since what Shechem did to me, he has been very kind, but I want to go home. I don't belong here."

They hugged and Levi said, "You know we will protect you. That's why we're here. Don't be afraid of what you see or hear. We'll meet you in a few minutes."

Staring suspiciously at them, she asked, "What are you going to do? We don't know these people and you know how father feels about conflict."

"Don't be concerned about that, Dinah," Simeon reassured her. "We know what we must do and believe that our God is with us. Just be ready to leave when we come back for you."

CHAPTER 5
CONSEQUENCES

Their action was swift and methodical. "Simeon and Levi...each took his sword and came boldly upon the city and killed all the males. And they killed Hamor and Shechem, his son with the edge of the sword, and took Dinah from Shechem's house, and went out." *(Genesis 34:25-26)*

Not only did they destroy the males, but they took "their sheep, their oxen, and their donkeys, what was in the city and what was in the field, and all their wealth. All their little ones and their wives they took captive; and they plundered even all that was in the houses." *(Genesis 34:28-29)*.

Seeing Dinah, Simeon and Levi returning home with an enormous procession of women, children, and livestock, their father, Jacob, panicked. Her mother, Leah, however, ran to her daughter and gently wiping the tears from her eyes, said, "Dinah, I'm relieved you are home now. No one will ever hurt you again and we'll never talk about this ordeal. It's as if it never happened."

Barely above a whisper and with her head hung very low, Dinah responded, "Yes, mother. We'll never talk about this again."

From that day forward, the once happy, carefree and adventurous Dinah retired to her tent, and ventured out only if necessary.

Jacob in the meantime, was terrified by his son's actions. Forgetting God's protection, he chastised them, saying, "You have troubled me...I am few in numbers, they [the surrounding cities] will gather themselves together against me and kill me. I shall be destroyed, my household and I."

Thinking first of their sister's safety, his sons responded, "Should he treat our sister like a harlot?" *(Genesis 34:30-31)*

Jacob never replied, nor did he look at or speak to his daughter again. Not knowing what to say, her brothers also avoided her.

Isolated and cloaked in shock, shame, and fear, Dinah spent the ensuing days and nights shrouded in darkness. She awoke oftentimes screaming in terror and shaking with fright. Her mind replayed Shechem's assault as if on automatic replay. Everything she thought and did sprouted from this brief encounter that now overshadowed her entire life. She, therefore, hid from the light of day, and feared the darkness of night. Drowning in a pain only she understood, she was dead yet alive. Her world was an endless internal and external torrent of scalding water drenching her body and soul. Past remembrances of happiness faded. There was no future. Only her present torment existed. Her life that was once marked with joy, adventure, and love, was turned upside down in one day.

Leah sat with her daily in silence. Feeling helpless and concerned for her daughter, her presence was all the comfort she could offer. Dinah's day and night quickly evolved into a dark, monotonous routine. Until approximately three months later, when she felt a tickling in her belly, followed by nausea and lightheadedness. Recognizing the signs, her mother cried out to her unseen God on behalf of her daughter. Knowing that there was now a new life growing within her, Dinah mustered the courage, and began calling on the name of the God of her fathers. She cried, day and night, looking up in surrendered hopelessness and desperation.

CHAPTER 6
DINAH'S DREAM

One night, instead of the dark nightmares that assaulted her sleep, she had a vivid, reality-like dream.

In the dream, *she had accidentally broken off a twig from a dry, dead bush. Picking it up from the ground, she closed her hand tightly around it, then crumbled it to dust. When she opened her hands, she was stunned to see the ashes sprouting green leaves. Afraid of what she saw, she flung it in the air. The ashes floated upward and disappeared into the clouds. Then as if returning from nowhere, she saw the ashes floating down and settled on the dead bush. Instantly, the bush grew and kept on growing until it became a gigantic, blooming tree, loaded with different kinds of low hanging, luscious, fruit.*

Sensing an unseen presence beside her, she awoke and said, *"I am that dry, twig, useful only to be grounded to ashes. But I know You are*

the God of my father, Jacob. You can do anything.
Here I am. I give my life to you, do with me
whatever you will."

The following day, Dinah felt hope
blooming in her heart. The baby growing in her
womb was no longer a reminder of her shame,
but a sign of new birth; new life emerging from
the ashes of her life.

Seeing a change in Dinah's countenance,
her mother said, "My daughter, something has
changed in you."

Dinah responded, "Yes mother, I believe
the God of my fathers' visited me in a dream a few
nights ago." She then related the dream to her
mother, who hung on to every word.

Then with tears overflowing her eyes, her
mother, shared, "Oh my child, the God of
Abraham, Isaac and your father has visited you.
I had a similar dream when I was carrying my
fourth son. That dream changed my perspective
and filled me with hope. All I could do was praise
my unseen God, so I named him PRAISE. That's
how Judah got his name. My daughter, I know

it's difficult now, but trust in God as I learned to do, and you will see that the best is yet to come."

With tears flowing down her joyful, yet sorrowful face, Dinah responded, "My baby is God's sign that He sees me and has a plan to bring forth new life out of my tragic experience; for that, I give thanks."

As her belly grew, so her heart expanded with hope. For the remainder of her pregnancy, Dinah sang over her child, and dedicated all future generations springing from her womb, to God's purposes. Six months later, she gave birth to a son as she took her final breath. Her mother named him, Sychar, meaning "End." For she said, *"My daughter's pain and suffering have finally ended in this place."*

Jacob and her family buried Dinah on "the parcel of land, where he had pitched his tent, from the children of Hamor, Shechem's father, for one hundred pieces of money." *(Genesis 33:19).* There, Jacob and his sons dug a well, and they named it "Jacob's well." It was adjacent to the city of Shechem, within walking distance to the place where his daughter was violated.

Leah then chose, Zari, a woman from among the captives from her son's raid against Shechem, to be his nursemaid. She was singularly devoted to Dinah throughout her confinement and they had become close friends. However, unknown to Leah, she was Shechem's sister, Sychar's aunt.

CHAPTER 7
SOWING BAD SEED

Zari cared for Sychar as if he were her own son. Benjamin, Jacob's youngest son, was less than a year older than Sychar and they grew together as brothers. While all Dinah's older brothers adopted her son as their little brother, it was Joseph who bonded more closely to Sychar, as he did to Benjamin.

On Sychar's sixth birthday, he asked, "Zari, who is my father? And where is my mother?"

Zari, who waited for the right time to share his lineage with her nephew, and the only remaining male of her family, answered, "One day, I'll tell you about your father, but not now. He was a brave man, Sychar, and was viciously killed before you were born but I know that he would have loved you very much. Both your father and his father were killed by wicked men. When you get older, I'll tell you the whole story.

Your mother was Joseph's sister, and she died when you were born."

"What was her name? And what was my father's name? Why did they both have to die? Did the same people kill them?" Asked the curious six-year old.

Zari pulled him closer and replied, "If I tell you your father's name, you will have to promise that you will never mention it to anyone here. Promise. Your mother's name was Dinah."

With childish sincerity, Sychar said, "I promise Zari. I will never mention his name."

Zari said, "Okay Sychar, I'm trusting you to never tell anyone. It's our secret. Your father's name was Shechem. He was my only brother. He was a brave and handsome prince, just like you."

Sychar eyes widened with wonder, and declared, "I'm a prince, Zari, just like my father?"

Hugging him, Zari said, "Yes, you are my son, you're a great prince, just like your father."

Zari initiated this conversation at least once a year, for the next seven years. On his thirteenth birthday, he asked, "Zari, I'm older now and want to know who those vicious people were who killed my father and mother."

Zari responded, "I've waited for this day for some time now Sychar, remember, your father was a prince and you are a prince also."

She then unleashed all the bitterness and hatred embedded in her heart for Jacob's two older sons, Simeon and Levi, and what they did to all the males in their village. Conspicuously missing from her account, was her brother's assault on his mother. When she was done sharing her version of what had transpired thirteen years prior, a seed of hatred and revenge was planted in Sychar's heart.

His only thought from that day forward, was avenging his father's death. He mentally killed them every day as his hatred and bitterness grew. When Zari died the following year, she made him promise to take vengeance against his father's murderers and carry on his lineage.

It was a promise he eagerly anticipated; one that replayed daily in his imagination. However, he knew that he had to wait for the right time and the right opportunity.

BOOK TWO

THE SONS OF JACOB

CHAPTER 1
BITTER ROOTS

Reminiscent of Jacob's earlier days, his current household mirrored similar division. This time, the chasm was between his older sons by his wife, Leah, and his younger son, Joseph, whose mother was Rachel. Clearly their father's undisputed favorite, Joseph was hated by his older brothers. With their family dysfunction reaching new heights, Jacob's older sons teemed with jealousy, rejection, resentment and murderous rage when Jacob proudly gave Joseph his colorful, one-of-a-kind, designer coat. To make matters worse, their hatred was further cemented after he shared his dreams that they would one day bow down to him.

It was therefore no surprise, when an opportunity arose to eliminate the favored son, that his brothers took full advantage. Seeing Joseph approaching as they were shepherding their sheep, they concocted a murderous plan.

Then, with unrestrained fury, they captured him and were prepared to strike, when one brother, Judah, intervened. Instead of killing him, he proposed, that they should sell him as a slave. Motivated by greed and hatred, the other brothers agreed. They stripped Joseph of his colorful coat and callously threw him into a nearby pit, then leisurely waited for the first slave traders to travel by.

Bewildered by his brothers' actions, and thinking they were playing a cruel joke, Joseph cried out from the pit. When there was no response, he cried even louder, calling each brother by name, "Reuben, Simeon, Levi, Zebulun, Issachar, Dan, Gad, and Asher, please stop this cruel joke. Get me out of this pit. I promise I won't tell father. Please."

Continuing to ignore his cries, Joseph pleaded with more urgency, "Brothers, please, please don't do this. I'm sorry for anything I've done to you. Please don't do this. I'm your brother."

There was no response, as the brothers ate lunch and waited.

Two hours went by as Joseph's cries transformed to agonizing pleas and groans. Still ignoring him, his brothers ate lunch and continued waiting for the slave traders. Simeon finally walked over to the pit and sneered, "Shut up, father isn't here to save you. You think you're so high and mighty with those dreams of yours. How dare you think that we will bow down to you. Not even in your dreams. Now we have you where you will bow down to us." Laughing sinisterly, he said between clenched teeth, "Bow down to us now, dreamer, and maybe we will pull you out."

Weak and fearful, Joseph continued pleading, "I'll do whatever you want. We're brothers, please, please, please don't do this."

Simeon barked, "So, what are you dreaming now, prince?" He then calmly strolled back to join his other brothers, just as a caravan of Ishmaelite traders passed by.

Judah led the negotiations with the traders while Simeon, Levi and two other brothers pulled Joseph out of the pit.

Levi said, "We're pulling you out. Take hold of the rope."

Joseph sighed with relief and said, "Oh brothers, I knew you wouldn't leave me here. I promise I won't tell father. It's as if it never happened."

Simeon snickered, and replied, "You're right, we'll make sure you won't tell father."

CHAPTER 2
LEADING QUESTION

As Joseph was lifted from the pit, his brothers threw him to the ground and tied his hands and feet. They then dragged him to the traders and made the exchange. Joseph continued pleading with them for mercy and reminding them that they were brothers. Even as the traders tied Joseph to their caravan, he cried out their names in agonizing pain. They in turn, walked away and headed in the opposite direction, never turning around or acknowledging his loud, heartbreaking cries.

On their return trip home, they devised a story to explain Joseph's absence. Smearing Joseph's coat with an animal's blood, they created the perfect subterfuge. Being the oldest, Reuben took the lead to talk to their father. Not wanting to lie, he lifted the blood-soaked coat and asked, "Father, is this the colorful coat you gave to your son, Joseph?"

Recognizing the coat, and seeing it covered with blood, Jacob jumped to the conclusion his sons had devised. He said, "It is my son's tunic, a wild beast has devoured him. Without doubt, Joseph is torn to pieces." Then Jacob tore his clothes, put sackcloth on his waist, and mourned for his son many days. And his entire household tried to comfort him; but he refused to be comforted and he said, "For I shall go down into the grave to my son in mourning." *(Genesis 37:33-35)*

Later that evening, the older sons gathered to congratulate themselves on their successful deception. Simeon, who was especially elated, said, "Reuben, what a brilliant performance. Father doesn't suspect a thing and you didn't have to lie."

Reuben responded, "It's the most difficult thing I've had to do. I fully intended to rescue him before you sold him. You know what we did was not right. We may have fooled father, but we didn't fool the God who sees."

Levi chimed in and said, "Well, God saw what we did to Shechem and his village and He protected us. He'll protect us now."

As he finished speaking, there was a rustling noise in a nearby bush. Simeon moved towards the sound and finding Benjamin and Sychar crouching behind it, he said, "Look who I found? Were you eavesdropping on us? How much did you hear?"

Benjamin responded and said, "We just got here and didn't hear much, just what Levi said. It makes no sense to us anyway."

Sychar added, "What Benjamin said is correct. We just got here and didn't understand anything that was said."

Simeon said threateningly, "Whatever you heard, don't tell father. If you do, we'll take care of you too, do you understand me?"

Both Benjamin and Sychar replied in terror, "Yes, we understand and won't say anything to father, promise. You can trust us."

They let the younger boys go and Reuben said, "I have a bad feeling that this will come back to haunt us one day."

Levi replied, "Not to worry, I'm sure Joseph is miles away by now. We'll never see him again."

That day, Benjamin and Sychar developed an inseparable and unbreakable bond. Conversely, a mutual distrust, dislike and suspicion emerged for the older brothers.

CHAPTER 3
FROM PRIDE TO HUMILITY

Even though Benjamin and Sychar never discussed the incident with their older brothers, they heard enough of the conversation to believe that Joseph might be alive. They, therefore, waited and watched for his return to confront and expose them.

As the years passed by, their hope faded. In the meantime, Jacob's ten older sons became a force to be reckoned with. They were feared wherever they went. They proudly referred to themselves as the sons of Israel [for their father's name had changed from Jacob to Israel] or Israelites. They feared no one, except their father.

Thirteen years after selling their brother into slavery, a famine hit their land. Jacob, therefore, sent his older sons to Egypt where they were told they could find food. Confident of a successful trip, they set out with their sacks filled with money, and their countenance overflowing with arrogance.

They found the grandeur and wealth of Egypt breathtaking. Staring in awe of its beauty, they travelled through the city to the marketplace where grain was sold. While standing in line to buy grain, Gad, one of the ten older brothers said, "Wow, this is incredible. One day, we will have a city bigger and greater than this. Its street will be gold and everyone will come to us for food."

Another brother, Dan, responded, "I can see it now. We will be dressed in royal robes and sit on ten magnificent thrones and rule the world."

Reuben replied, "Ten, why ten. We are eleven brothers."

Simeon retorted, "I agree with Dan, it's ten, Joseph is no more, and who can trust Benjamin?"

Levi said, "If God grants us to expand as our father tells us we will, then it has to be all or none. Remember, we're one family now, not two divided."

Ignoring his comment, they continued advancing in line until it was their turn. Reuben, who was usually the spokesperson, prepared to take the lead. As they approached the Egyptian lord of the land, they bowed low in reverence. Then rising before him, Reuben began to speak and was immediately silenced by a sharp poke in his back by one of the guards.

Glaring at the ten of them with transparent suspicion, the Egyptian lord took the lead and asked in a harsh tone, "Where do you come from?" *(Genesis 42:7)*

Intimidated by his disapproving countenance, they said in unison, "From the land of Canaan to buy food." *(Genesis 42:7)*

Continuing to glare at them, the lord shouted accusingly, "You are spies! You have come to see the nakedness of the land!" *(Genesis 42:9)*

For the first time in their lives, the ten brothers trembled with fear and humbly, said, "No, my lord, but your servants have come to buy food. We are all one man's sons; we are honest men; your servants are not spies." *(Genesis 42:10-11)*

Enjoying seeing the ten men squirm under his scrutiny, the lord continued his vigorous accusations, "No, but have come to see the nakedness of the land." *(Genesis 42:12)*

Becoming visibly nervous, they all began to mumble, "Your servants are twelve brothers, the sons of one man in the land of Canaan; and in fact, the youngest is with our father today, and one is no more." *(Genesis 42:13)*

The lord paused while still glaring at the ten men, who were now visibly shaking with fright. Speaking even more harshly and deliberately, he barked, "It is as I spoke to you, saying, 'You are spies!' In this manner you shall be tested: By the life of Pharaoh, you shall not leave this place unless your youngest brother comes here. Send one of you, and let him bring your brother; and you shall be kept in prison, that your words may be tested to see whether there is any truth in you; or else, by the life of Pharaoh, surely you are spies!" *(Genesis 42:14-15)*

He then ordered the guards to take them to prison and walked away.

CHAPTER 4
UNRAVELED

For the next three days, the ten brothers languished in prison fearing their fate. The lord visited them on the third day and said, "Do this and live, for I fear God: If you are honest men, let one of your brothers be confined to the prison; but you, go and carry grain for the famine of your houses. And bring your youngest brother to me; so your words will be verified, and you shall not die." *(Genesis 42:20)*

Upon hearing this ultimatum, their hearts raced with fear. They were speechless as they stared at each other, while contemplating their fate and the future of their family. In a tone dripping with dread, guilt and condemnation, they confessed to each other in their native language, saying, "We are truly guilty concerning our brother, for we saw the anguish of his soul when he pleaded with us, and we would not hear;

therefore, this distress has come upon us."
(Genesis 42:21)

Adding more reproach and blame, Reuben spewed out in anger, "Did I not speak to you, saying, 'do not sin against the boy;' and you would not listen". Therefore behold, his blood is now required of us." *(Genesis 42:22)*

They continued accusing and blaming each other for their past sins and current predicament. Understanding their dialect, the lord turned away attempting to restrain his emotions. Humbled by the unlimited power his God had granted him to make life and death decisions, he inhaled deeply, while thinking of his next move.

Slowly and deliberately, he walked before them as they fully prostrated themselves before him in surrendered reverence. Granting them permission to stand before him, he decided to soften his approach. He then divulged that he would release nine of them, and keep one in prison, pending their return with the youngest brother.

Then slowly marching before them, and glaring at each, while mumbling to himself, "Umm...now which one should I keep in prison?"

Stopping in front of Simeon, he gave the command to bound him in chains and return him to the cells.

Crumbling at his feet, Simeon pleaded, "Sir, please, please, I beg you, let me return with my brothers."

The lord turned away from his pleas, nodded to the guards who grabbed Simeon by the arm and marched him away. Simeon, who was one of the most impetuous, arrogant and ruthless of the ten brothers, cried out in anguish as he was being separated from his brothers. Levi, his partner in crime, also cried loudly as they took him away.

As the eldest brother, Reuben, tried to manage the situation and said, "We will come back for you. I will convince father to let us bring Benjamin back. Don't be afraid, we won't be separated."

The Egyptian lord understood what Reuben had said and commanded them to leave immediately. They responded without hesitation fearing they might anger him further, mounted their donkeys and left. However, as they stopped to feed their animals along the way, one brother discovered that his money was still in his sack. Alarmed, he shouted in agonizing terror, "My money has been restored, and there it is, in my sack!" *(Genesis 42:28)*

Unknown to them the lord had commanded his guards to not only give the brothers grain but to also restore their money.

The same proud and arrogant men on their way to Egypt, crumbled in fear and despair on their way home. They nervously looked around to see if they were being chased by the Egyptians; fearing that they may be accused of stealing the grain. Not taking any chances, they anxiously mounted their donkeys and fled away like scared rabbits. Trembling with terror, they mumbled to one another, "What is this that God has done to us?" *(Genesis 42:28)*

CHAPTER 5
FEARS EXPOSED

The brother's faces were white with fright when they arrived home. Seeing his once fearsome, bullying sons trembling as they dismounted their donkeys, and noticing one son missing, their father, Israel asked, "What happened? Where's Simeon?"

Amazed to see their usually intimating older brothers shaking with fear, Benjamin and Sychar stared in shock. Exchanging glances, they were excited to hear what caused their fright.

Reuben was the first to regain composure and shared, "The man who is lord of the land spoke roughly to us, and took us for spies of the country. But we said to him, 'we are honest men; we are not spies. We are twelve brothers, sons of our father; one is no more, and the youngest is with our father this day in the land of Canaan.'

Then the man, the lord of the country, said to us, 'By this I will know that you are honest men: Leave one of your brothers here with me, take food for the famine for your households, and be gone. And bring your youngest brother to me; so I shall know that you are not spies, but that you are honest men. I will grant your brother to you, and you may trade in the land.'" *(Genesis 42:33-34)*

Israel, who was now an old man, avoided conflict at all costs. He fell to the ground, despairing of life. Benjamin helped him to his feet and steadied him on his arms. Jacob then said, "Let's go inside the tent. I'm sure there's more to this story and I want to hear everything. No deceptions."

The brothers proceeded to unload their donkeys before heading in. As they did, all of them noticed that their money was back in their sack. Fear gripped their hearts even more. Knowing his older sons, Israel groaned, "You have bereaved me: Joseph is no more. Simeon is no more, and you want to take Benjamin. All these things are against me." *(Genesis 42:36)*

Seizing the opportunity to regain his father's good graces, [for Reuben had slept with one of his father's concubines], Reuben said, "Kill my two sons if I do not bring him back to you; put him in my hands, and I will bring him back to you."

Not trusting Reuben, Israel said, "My son shall not go down with you, for his brother is dead, and he is left alone. If any calamity should befall him along the way in which you go, then you would bring down my grey hair with sorrow to the grave." *(Genesis 42:38)*

Israel then drew Benjamin closer and said, "You are the only son I have left of your mother, Rachel. I can't bear losing you."

Benjamin hugged his father and said, "I don't mind going father, if it means we will get more grain. It's better than all of us dying from starvation."

With cautious optimism, Israel said "Perhaps the famine will end soon and we won't need more grain. Let's see how it goes."

Later that evening, Benjamin said to Sychar, "Whatever happened in Egypt is a good thing. I've never seen my brothers afraid of anything. Whoever the lord of the land is, I want to meet him."

Sychar replied, "Me too, somehow I think he's our missing link."

As they parted, Sychar thought to himself, *I hope they do go back without Benjamin and the lord of the land kills them all. It will save me the pleasure of doing it myself. But, however God chooses to avenge my father and his family is fine with me, as long as I see them fall.*

CHAPTER 6
RETURNING TO EGYPT

Later, as the famine became more severe and there was no grain left, Israel said to his older sons, "Go back, buy us a little food." *(Genesis 43:2)*

His son Judah spoke to him, saying, "The man solemnly warned us, saying, 'You shall not see my face unless your brother is with you.' If you send our brother with us, we will go down and buy you food. But if you will not send him, we will not go down; for the man said to us, 'You shall not see my face unless your brother is with you.'" *(Genesis 43:3-5)*

Israel asked accusingly, "Why did you deal so wrongfully with me as to tell the man whether you had still another brother?" *(Genesis 43:6)*

Trying to cover their tracks, the other brothers chimed in, and deceiving their father, said, "The man asked us pointedly about ourselves and our family, saying 'Is your father

74

still alive? Have you another brother?' And we told him according to these words. Could we possibly have known that he would say, 'Bring your brother down?" *(Genesis 43:7)*

Listening intently to their conversation, Benjamin added, "Father, I don't object going. If the man wants to meet me, then I will go. I am not afraid. In fact, I'm intrigued as to why he wants to meet me."

Wanting to affirm Benjamin and convince their father to let him go, Judah offered himself as a sacrifice. He pleaded with his father, "Send the lad with me, and we will arise and go, that we may live and not die, both we and you and our little ones. I, myself, will be surety for him, from my hand you shall require him. If I do not bring him back to you and set him before you, then let me bear the blame forever. For if we had not lingered, surely by now we would have returned this second time." *(Genesis 43:8-10)*

Finally conceding, Israel said, "If it must be so, then do this: Take some of the best fruits of the land in your vessels and carry down a present for the man ~ a little balm and a little honey,

spices and myrrh, pistachio nuts and almonds. Take double money in your hand, and take back in your hand the money that was returned...perhaps it was an oversight. Take your brother also, and arise, go back to the man. And may God Almighty give you mercy before the man, that he may release your other brother and Benjamin. If I am bereaved, I am bereaved!"
(Genesis 43:11-14)

Without hesitation, the ten brothers left to return to Egypt, praying with fear and trembling the entire way.

CHAPTER 7

UNHINGHED

Before leaving with his brothers, Benjamin confessed to Sychar, "I'm actually more afraid of my brothers than meeting the lord of the land. If I don't come back, Sychar, I want you to have my inheritance. Since Joseph left, you have been my true brother and I want you to have a share in everything that is mine. Father didn't want to discuss it, but he agreed."

Sychar replied, "Based on what they shared, I think they are the ones who should be fearful of you, because if they don't bring you to the man, their life is in danger. From my vantage point, you have the upper hand in this, so don't let them intimidate you."

Benjamin said, "I didn't see it that way. I think you're right. Anyway, I'm excited to be going, even though leaving father is difficult. I know you'll watch over him while I'm gone."

"He's in good hands, Benjamin. Not to worry," said Sychar, as they parted.

No sooner had they left, when Levi said, "Benjamin, whatever you do, do not tell the man anything more about us. We're in enough trouble as it is. We will bow down to him, and whatever he says, we will do. He's an extremely powerful man. We are as grasshoppers in his sight. He has the power to destroy us so it's important that we make a better impression this time. We will present you to him to prove that we are honest men and give him the gifts from our father. Hopefully, he'll release Simeon to us."

Benjamin said in awe, "Wow, he must be a very powerful ruler. I can't wait to meet him."

Levi chimed in and said, "Remember, he's not one of us. He's Egyptian and they have different customs. Whatever he says, just do it even if it's different from what we're used to doing. We must win his favor; our lives depend on it."

As soon as they arrived in Egypt and stood before the lord of the land, they immediately prostrated themselves, and stayed prostrated, until he told them to rise. When they did, with bowed heads, Reuben said, "Sir, we have returned with our youngest brother as you asked. We have also returned double the money for the grain you gave us and presents from our father."

"When the lord saw Benjamin with them, he said to the steward of his house, "Take these men to my home, and slaughter an animal and make ready; for these men will dine with me at noon." *(Genesis 43:17)*

"The men were afraid because they were brought into the lord's house; and they said, "It is because of the money, which was returned in our sacks the first time, that we are brought in, so that he may make a case against us and seize us, to take us as slaves with our donkeys." *(Genesis 43:18)*

The brothers, except Benjamin, became unhinged. Finding the first person they could appeal to, they pleaded their case, hoping they would not be taken in captivity. The lord's servant listened and said, "Peace be with you, do not be afraid. Your God and the God of your father has given you treasure in your sacks."

Then he brought Simeon out to them." *(Genesis 43:23)*

The servant then led them to the lord's house where they anxiously waited. While they waited, they asked Simeon about his experience in the prison. Simeon shared, "I was in an isolated cell. The only person I saw was the man who brought my food. I've had plenty of time to think and believe this is because of what we did to our brother."

Benjamin, who was sitting near Simeon, asked, "What did you do to Joseph?"

Simeon replied, "We did something terrible and I'm sorry for what we did. Please forgive me." And with tears, he begged for Benjamin's forgiveness.

"Forgive you for what? What did you do to my brother. I've always suspected that you lied to father about him. Tell me the truth now or I will tell the man that I'm not Benjamin and we'll all die."

Just as Simeon was about to respond, the lord arrived, and they "bowed down before him to the earth." *(Genesis 43:26)* Simeon, however,

completely prostrated himself and stayed
prostrated until the lord granted him permission
to rise.

CHAPTER 8
FALSE SECURITY

Bracing themselves for the lord's wrath and imminent death, they were shocked when he instead asked about their father's welfare. They answered, "Your servant our father is in good health and he is still alive." And they bowed their heads down and prostrated themselves [again]." *(Genesis43:28)*

The lord then saw Benjamin and asked, "Is this your younger brother of whom you spoke to me?"

Benjamin nodded. The lord replied, "God be gracious to you, my son." He then quickly left the room to restrain himself. When he returned, he instructed his servants to seat them at the table according to their birth age, from the oldest to the youngest.

The brothers looked at each other in utter astonishment, wondering how the lord knew their ages. He then commanded his servants to serve

Benjamin five times more than the others. Several times throughout the evening, Benjamin caught the lord staring at him. On one occasion, he summed up the courage to stare back, and was amazed to see familiar eyes he thought he recognized.

The lord then commanded his servants to give the brothers as much food as they could carry and return the money they had given back in their sacks. He also instructed them to put a special silver cup, in Benjamin's bag. The following morning, the brothers rode off, relieved that they were leaving unharmed. However, no sooner had they left the city, when they heard an army approaching.

CHAPTER 9
THE SILVER CUP

With their confidence soaring since their positive encounter with the Egyptian lord, the brothers ignored the army following closely behind. They were therefore shocked, when the army pulled alongside and demanded that they stop. The Egyptian commander halted the Israelites, and asked, "Why have you repaid evil for good?" *(Genesis 44:4)*

He then continued accusing them of stealing a silver cup belonging to the lord; a unique cup with which he practiced "sorcery." *(Genesis 44:5)* The brothers were stunned with fear and began trembling with fright.

They answered, "Why does my lord say these words? Far be it from us that your servants should do such a thing. Look, we brought back to you from the land of Canaan the money which we found in the mouth of our sacks. How then could we steal silver or gold from your lord's house?" *(Genesis 44:8)*

Feeling confident that this was a gross mistake, they further added, "With whomever of your servants it is found, let him die, and we also will be my lord's slaves." *(Genesis 44:9)*

The commander responded, "Now also let it be according to your words; he with whom it is found shall be my slave, and you shall be blameless." *(Genesis 44:10)*

They proceeded to search everyone's belongings and to their horror, the cup was found in Benjamin's sack. Crying out in anguish and panic, his brothers fell before the commander. Benjamin, however, stared at the cup as if seeing a ghost. Daring to believe the impossible, he inhaled deeply as his heart raced with excitement.

They returned to the lord's house where they [again] fell prostrate before him in complete surrender. Playing cat and mouse with them, the lord asked, "What deed is this you have done? Did you not know that such a man as I can certainly practice divination?" *(Genesis 44:15)*

Judah replied, "What shall we say to my lord? What shall we speak? Or how shall we clear ourselves? God has found out the iniquity of your servants; here we are, my lord's slaves, both we and he also with whom the cup was found." *(Genesis 44:16)*

Continuing his taunting, the lord, responded, "Far be it from me that I should do so; the man in whose hand the cup was found he shall be my slave. And as for you, go up in peace to your father." *(Genesis 44:17)*

With their composure completely unraveled, Judah fell to the ground at the lord's feet. Groveling before him, with tears and groaning, he pleaded with the lord to reconsider his decision. After recounting the reasons he could not return home without Benjamin, he offered himself as a sacrifice.

Finding it difficult to maintain an indifferent composure, the lord commanded his servants to leave the room. When they did, he stepped down toward them and said, "I am Joseph; does my father still live?" *(Genesis 44:3)*

Overcome with shock and even greater fear, the older brothers stumbled backwards over themselves. Benjamin, however, smiled and approached his brother.

Seeing their stunned, frightened countenance, Joseph said, "...do not be angry with yourselves because you sold me here; for God sent me before you to preserve life. So it was not you who sent me here but God, and He has made me a father to Pharaoh, and lord of all his house, and a ruler throughout all the land of Egypt." *(Genesis 44:5)*

Still frozen in guilt, shame and fear, the brothers were, for the first time in their lives, scared speechless. They stared at Joseph as if seeing a ghost. Joseph then "fell on his brother Benjamin's neck and wept, and Benjamin wept on his neck. Moreover, he kissed all his brothers and wept over them, and after that his brothers talked with him." *(Genesis 44:15)*

CHAPTER 10
REUNITED

Benjamin couldn't wait to speak alone with Joseph. After his brothers left to prepare for their return trip home, Benjamin seized the opportunity to talk to him. With exuberant joy, he said, "I hoped it was you, Joseph. The entire trip here, I wondered why an important lord in Egypt insisted on meeting me. Oh Joseph, I missed you and have so much to share with you."

Joseph hugged him again and again, and said, "I missed you too little brother. And I missed father. How is he, really? Not sure I can trust what the others told me. Let me look more closely at you, you're all grown up now. Do you have a wife, any children? I want to know all."

Benjamin replied, "And I can't wait to learn about you. I'm so, so sorry for what they did to you Joseph. Father's heart was broken when they led him to believe that you were killed by a wild animal. They brought your colorful coat to him covered with blood and he assumed you were killed. Oh, Joseph, we've missed you so much and I still can't believe you're here." He then shouted, "My brother is alive. He's alive, I can't wait to tell father and Sychar."

After hugging again, Joseph asked, "And how is my nephew Sychar? I can't wait to see him too. I want him to have a full inheritance of everything God has given me."

Overflowing with things to share, Benjamin said, "It was when I saw the silver cup in my sack that I knew. It looked just like the cup you told me our mother drank from because she believed it had magical powers. Did you make a replica because I still have the one we played with? And you should have seen the others faces when they saw the cup in my sack. They turned white with fright because they knew they dared not return home without me. And I'm sure they felt certain that you would kill all of us. Oh, Joseph, there's so much I want to share."

Joseph replied, "And there's a lot I want to share with you as well. I can't wait for you to meet my two sons. You never told me if you're married and have any children? And what about Sychar? Is he married too? Well, I guess I'll find out in a few weeks when you return with father. I'll prepare special places near me for you and Sychar. But you must go now, there's lots of work ahead."

Benjamin hugged him again and asked, "You're really real right? I'm not dreaming, you're really my brother, Joseph?"

Joseph gave him a friendly brotherly slap on the head and said, "Here, pinch me. I'm real. Now let's go."

Unashamed to be seen hugging his brother, the Egyptian lord and Benjamin walked out, arm in arm, both with tears flowing down their faces.

CHAPTER 11
THE RIDE HOME

Benjamin chattered excitedly all the way home. His brothers, however, were deadly silent. Reuben finally broke their silence and said, "God has indeed been gracious to us. Joseph had it in his power to do whatever he wanted with us, and yet he chose to forgive us. We don't deserve such mercy?"

Judah added, "I'm still shocked. Remember the dreams he shared. God made his dreams come true. Not only did we bow to him several times, but the entire world bows to him. I still can't believe it, but I'm so thankful that he is alive. Our brother is alive."

Simeon, finally finding his voice, said sobbing uncontrollably, "He showed me such kindness while I was in prison. Now I know why. I don't deserve his kindness. When I think of how we treated him. The unkind things I said. Oh, God, please forgive me, please forgive me."

Seeing his remorse, the other brothers began sobbing as well, crying out to God for forgiveness. Benjamin, who was the only one composed said, "Joseph has been more honorable than all of us. He has forgiven you. Didn't you hear him say that it was God's plan all along."

Judah replied, through tears, "Yes, God took our evil actions and used it for good. What kind of God is this?"

Levi, who was still regaining his composure said, "It's more than we could ever deserve. Only God knows how to humble us. Let's all agree, that we will never, ever, from this generation and all generations to come, that we will not tear each other apart. Let's instill this in our children now."

Benjamin, who was intently observing and listening said, "Do you really mean that, or are you just saying it because you have been exposed and now have to face father's wrath?"

Asher replied, "We deserve his wrath and I'm ready to face whatever consequences."

Dan added, "Umm...Joseph has shown so much kindness to us. I wonder if this will change after we bring father to Egypt. You know how close they were."

For the first time in his life, Benjamin confronted his brothers and said, "You just won't learn, will you? When will this jealousy and envy stop? Father loves all of us and shows it in different ways. And, yes, he especially loves Joseph and I understand why. Stop thinking about yourselves and start considering father. I can't believe you're suspicious of what Joseph will do to you after he sees father. He can do anything he wants to you even now, and could have when we were in Egypt. How dare you speak evil of him after what you all did?"

Reuben said, "I agree with Benjamin. Let's stop this division between us and finally be brothers. We are all Jacob's sons, Israelites, and we're proud of it. When we relocate to Egypt, staying together as one large family will be essential."

Judah added, "Let's not forget father's dream that he shares with us all the time. God is building a nation with us. We must have one identity."

Levi chimed in, "Yes, we must share a common experience that binds us together with our God. If this doesn't do it, I don't know what will."

CHAPTER 12

SHOCKING NEWS

Reflecting on their experience in Egypt, and humbled by Joseph's kindness and forgiveness, the brothers braced themselves to meet their father. Reuben again elected to lead the conversation, and as the eldest brother, decided to take responsibility for everything that transpired.

Anxious for his sons return, Isracl had set servants to watch for their coming. Even though well advance in age, when he was told that they were approaching, Israel, with assistance from Sychar, walked out to greet them.

Benjamin, elated to share the news of his brother's stature and presence in Egypt, ignored Reuben, dismounted his donkey and ran full speed ahead. Yelling as he ran, "Joseph is alive! Joseph is alive! I've seen him. Joseph is alive."

Israel's heart stood still and hugged Benjamin, saying, "Thank God, who returned you

to me." Not comprehending what Benjamin
shouted as he ran, he waited for his other sons to
ensure that they had all returned. When he saw
all of them he asked, "What's this that Benjamin
is shouting?"

"They told him, saying, "Joseph is still
alive, and he is governor over all the land of
Egypt." His heart stood still again because he did
not believe them." *(Genesis 45:27)*

Catching his breath, he then asked, "Is
this true? Is my son, my Joseph, still alive? He
wasn't killed by an animal? Is it really true?"

Benjamin watched closely to see how they
responded. Reuben cleared his throat and said,
"Yes father, Joseph is still alive. He was not
killed by an animal. There's more that we have to
tell you, but let's go in and we will share
everything."

"Seeing the carts which Joseph had sent to
carry him, the spirit of Jacob (Israel) their father
revived. Then Israel said, "It is enough, Joseph
my son is still alive. I will go and see him before I
die." *(Genesis 44:27-28)*

Sychar ran to Benjamin and said, "I'm so glad you're back and can't wait to hear everything; especially about Joseph and how he got to Egypt."

Hearing Sychar's comment to Benjamin, Israel asked, "Let's go inside. I can't wait to hear how my son, my Joseph, got to Egypt and how he's become a great and wealthy man. I can't wait to see him. Let's celebrate, for my son, whom I thought was dead, and is alive."

After his sons unpacked the food from Egypt, Jacob asked a servant to pour the wine. Raising his cup, he thanked God for allowing him to see his son, Joseph, again. Then he asked, "Now, tell me all about my son and how he got to Egypt."

CHAPTER 13
TRUE CONFESSIONS

Reclining on his cushion, Israel declared, "This is one of the greatest days of my life. My son, Joseph is still alive. Sons, tell me all about how he got to Egypt. I'm too excited to wait to hear it from him myself. I thought he was surely dead when you showed me his coat. I was too distraught to ask at the time, but where did you find his coat and I assumed you looked for his body and didn't find it. Tell me what happened."

Reuben cleared his throat and said, "Father, we beg your forgiveness, your son was never killed by an animal."

Managing to jump to his feet, Israel exclaimed, "What? Then how did the blood get all over his coat?"

Clearing his throat again, Reuben answered, "We deceived you into thinking that he was killed by an animal, father. Please forgive us.

We sold him into slavery to Ishmaelite slave traders."

Israel fell back into his cushion, groaning in agony. Finally regaining composure, he rambled on, "All these years you led me to believe that my son was dead. You deceived me all these years. How could you? My life has been one deceit after another. Oh, God, how long must I pay for my sins? Why did you deceive me into thinking my son was killed? Why did you sell your own brother into slavery? You are heartless. Oh, God help us. Help us to become one family. You promised that we will be one nation, with one God. How, God of my fathers? How, when we cannot even be a family of twelve sons right now? Oh, my sons, what made you sin against God, your brother and me? What?"

Silence permeated the room as the brothers were without answers. Then, one by one, each son apologized to Israel and promised that they had learned their lesson. Israel stared at each in disbelief shaking his head.

Levi summed up the courage and said, "Joseph has forgiven us father. We hope you can to. He believes that God sent him ahead to Egypt to save our family. As to how he ended up as the lord of the land, we don't know. God divinely placed him there. There is much we need to discover about our brother."

Judah added, "He wants us to come and live in Egypt. As lord of the land, he can give us any land he chooses. There's plenty of food there, for our entire household."

Processing what he heard, Israel said, "Deception has got to end in our family. I forgive you, because I need to be forgiven for deception in my life as well. How can I hold this against you? I don't know how our God will unite us, but I know He will because He promised my grandfather Abraham, that his seed would become a great nation. He also promised my father and he promised me. So far, He has kept all His promises to us."

Enjoying seeing their older brothers drowning in humility, Benjamin and Sychar smiled at each other. Benjamin said, "Father, I guessed it was Joseph who was the lord of the land. He had hidden one of our mother's silver cups in my sack. It was a similar cup Joseph used to tell me stories about her. He wanted me to know that it was him."

His brother glared at him in stunned silence. Simeon then commented, "So that's why you didn't panic when you saw the cup? Why didn't you tell us?"

Benjamin said, "Even if I did, you were all so afraid, I'm sure you wouldn't believe me. Besides, only Joseph and I knew about the cup?"

Israel added, "I know exactly what silver cup you're referring to, but I thought I had thrown it away some time ago, even before Joseph left us."

Benjamin said, "You did throw it away, but Joseph rescued it and hid it under his bed cushion. It was our secret. I have it now. I've kept it under my cushion ever since he left. It reminds me of him. I'll get it."

He ran from the room and in a few minutes returned with a tarnished, silver cup that looked like the one found in his sack. Once again, his brothers looked dazed upon seeing the cup in Benjamin's hands.

Israel said, "Bring it to me."

When he did, Israel said, "Thank God Joseph rescued this cup. But I want no more deception and no more secrets in our family. I will keep this and return it to Joseph. I'm sure he will want it back. Besides, I want to give him something when I see him. He will treasure this, as it will remind him of his mother."

Sometime later, his entire household, "sixty-six persons in all," *(Genesis 46-26)*, entered the land of Goshen, where they settled in Egypt. Israel finally held his beloved son, Joseph, in his arms. For the first time in a long time, he felt complete.

CHAPTER 14
FATHER AND SON

Israel held on to his son that he thought was dead, but was alive. He embraced him and smeared his face with kisses. He would look at him again, and start embracing and kissing him all over again. Both Israel and Joseph's faces were soaked with tears. When Israel finally found his voice, he said, "Joseph, my son, my boy, my precious son. God has indeed been good to this old and broken man, for the son I thought was lost, is alive and well."

Joseph, still unable to talk, simply embraced his father and said, "Father, father, how I have longed for this day. I saw it, and it is now here."

"Son," said Israel, "I'm so sorry for what you have endured. God shall yet make a family of us. I don't know how or when, but I know He will. He promised and I have learned to trust in His promises."

"All is forgiven, father," said Joseph, "For I know that God sent me ahead of my family to make a way for us to do exactly that. Let me look at you. It's been some time since I last saw you."

Israel bowed his head and said, "I have aged a great deal since you last saw me. I am proud of every line and every wrinkle. Each tells its own story." Then pointing to the deep crevices on his forehead, he said, "These are particularly precious to me, for it reflects my deep pain and sorrow when I was led to believe that you were killed by a wild animal." Then pointing to other deeply embedded lines on his cheeks, he said, "And these, these are when I lost your mother, even before she died."

Changing the subject, he said, "Speaking of your mother, I brought you her silver up. I know how much you treasured it. How clever of you to put it in Benjamin's sack. But son, I trust that you don't follow in your mother's footsteps of divination, idolatry and sorcery. Our God is One God. We cannot add anything to Him, nor can we take anything away from Him."

Joseph smiled to himself and responded, "Yes, that was clever of me. I made a replica only to remind myself of her. Father, I've met the God of our fathers. He was with me the entire time I was away. He is the One who prospered everything I did and protected me. On days when I would give up, He encouraged me, gave me strength to continue and assured me that He was with me. I know there is no other God beside Him. I would not add or take away anything. He IS exactly who He IS."

Reaching to hug and kiss him again, Jacob said, "Now that I've seen and held you, I'm ready to go to my fathers and my dear wife, Leah. In fact, I want to be buried next to her, in the same cave where my fathers were buried."

"Not so soon father," Joseph remarked, "I'm not ready to let you go, besides you haven't met my two sons, Manasseh and Ephraim."

"I know my days are numbered, son," said Israel. "God has given me a very full life. He told me that you shall receive a double portion inheritance, a portion for each of your sons."

Joseph wept.

CHAPTER 15
THE END OF A LEGEND

Knowing his days were ending, Israel gave each of his sons his final blessings, but to Joseph, he gave a double portion, to include his two sons. He then instructed his sons to bury him "with my fathers...in the land of Canaan, which Abraham bought...There they buried Abraham and Sarah his wife, there they buried Isaac and Rebekah his wife, and there I buried Leah." Within a short time, he breathed his last, with his son, Joseph, at his side.

Planning for the most important experience of his life, Joseph organized his father's burial. It was the most spectacular event Egypt had ever seen. Greater than the burial of any before him, Israel was honored with the burial of a mighty king.

"So, Joseph went up to bury his father; and with him went up all the servants of Pharaoh, the elders of his house, and all the elders of the land of Egypt, as well as all the house of Joseph, his brothers, and his father's house......And there went up with him both chariots and horsemen and it was a very great gathering." *(Genesis 50:7-9).*

As his funeral procession passed through the land of his enemies, and his father's enemies, the Canaanites stopped in awe and wonder. Believing it was the burial of a great Egyptian, they declared, "This is a deep mourning of the Egyptians." And they honored the man being buried by naming the place of their mourning, "Abel Mizraim, [meaning 'mourning of Egypt'] which is beyond the Jordan." *(Genesis 50:11)*

CHAPTER 16
LIVING THE DREAM

With their father gone, Joseph's older brothers felt even guiltier, ashamed and afraid. They said, "Perhaps Joseph will hate us, and may actually repay us for all the evil which we did to him." Reverting to their old habits of deception, they concocted a story to protect themselves.

Afraid to speak to their brother directly, they sent messengers, saying, "Before your father died he commanded, saying, thus you shall say to Joseph: I beg you, please forgive the trespass of your brothers and their sin, for they did evil to you. Now please, forgive the trespass of the servants of the God of your father." *(Genesis 50:17-18)*

Joseph, however, wept when he heard the message. His brothers were unable to trust his kindness, and because their own hearts were evil, they needed reassurance of his protection. They also, went and fell [again] before his face, and said, "Behold, we are your servants."

Joseph said to them, "Do not be afraid, for am I in the place of God? But as for you, you meant evil against me, but God meant it for good, to bring it about as it is this day, to save many people alive. Now therefore, do not be afraid; I will provide for you and your little ones." And he comforted them and spoke kindly to them. *(Genesis 50:19-21)*

After the mourning period for his father ended, Joseph felt it was the right time to share his story with his family. Feeling emotionally prepared to expose his heart and his past, he invited his entire family to join him for a special celebration. Without knowing the purpose of the celebration, his brothers and their families eagerly anticipated the joyful event.

With the table set and the feast prepared, everyone gathered. After laughter and conversation, Joseph stood up, and everyone immediately stopped whatever he or she was doing. He allowed a moment of silence as all eyes were fixed on him in awe. He then cleared his throat and began to articulate the most incredible story they ever heard.

CHAPTER 17
AN INCREDIBLE STORY
FAITH

Wanting to cover his older brothers' evil actions, he said, "It began when I was carried away by slave traders. I cried out for my family, and then I began crying out for the God of our fathers."

Deliberately looking at his older brothers, he said, "Brothers, you know I'm a dreamer. That first night I had a reality-like dream that recurred intermittently over the next few years, especially on days when I felt most discouraged. In this dream, *I accidentally broke off a branch from a dry, dead bush. Picking it up from the ground, I looked at the dead, broken branch, and was stunned to see it sprouting leaves, flowers and fruit. I stared at the branch in wonder and unbelief, but could not deny what I saw. Feeling afraid of holding this living, growing branch, I flung it in the air. The branch floated upward and disappeared into the clouds. I stared as the branch floated upward. Then as if returning from nowhere, the branch floated down and reattached itself to the dead bush. The bush grew and kept on growing until it became a gigantic, blooming tree, loaded with different kinds of low hanging, luscious fruit.*

I knew our God was reassuring me through the dream that I shall one day be reconnected to my family. When I awoke, an incredible peace and unexplainable presence enveloped me. It was the most amazing feeling I ever had. One day I was distraught, and the next, an unseen presence came beside me, inside me and all around me. I knew that everything was going to be alright."

His son Manasseh, knowing never to interrupt his father, impetuously asked, "Father, but why were you sold into slavery?"

Looking directly at his brothers, he said, "The people who sold me had planned evil against me, but it is evident today, that God used it for a great purpose, and for that I'm grateful."

Knowing not to probe further, his son sat quietly, fixated on every word his father spoke. Joseph continued. "On the journey to the slave market, the presence kept assuring me that God was with me, that no matter what happened, I was to trust in the God of my fathers. I was later sold to an Egyptian man named Potiphar, who was a captain of Pharaoh's army. I listened carefully and paid attention to their customs and within a short time I learned their language. Because father taught me to manage his property, and I knew how to take inventory, I made a few suggestions to improve managing the estate.

It's as if this unseen presence told me what to say and what to do. I knew I was never alone. Whatever my God told me, I did and because of that, everything I did was successful. Before long, I was promoted as overseer of all Potiphar's property. He trusted me completely and God blessed his household to become very great under my management."

CHAPTER 18
AN INCREDIBLE STORY
INTEGRITY

Pausing to clear his throat, Joseph continued, "Potiphar's wife, however, wanted me to be her personal slave, if you know what I mean. She hounded me day after day to lie with her and I refused. How could I do this great wickedness, and sin against God?" *(Genesis 39:9)*.

Joseph shook his head. "She was relentless. After all, I am handsome and irresistible, don't you think?" Everyone laughed hilariously, nodding in agreement as the mood in the room shifted and his older brothers visibly relaxed.

His wife chimed in and said, "Yes, definitely handsome and irresistible."

Joseph smiled and continued, "His wife watched my every move. She finally found me alone, and tried to force me to sleep with her, but

I ran. However, she managed to grab my coat as I ran. Then she began screaming and accusing me of trying to assault her. What could I do, but trust God? I was after all a slave and she was my master's wife."

His brother's and son's eyes widened with horror as they listened intently to Joseph's story.

"My master gave me a life sentence and threw me in prison. Nonetheless, the unseen presence assured me again and again that He was with me and that everything would be all right. Little did I know then, the greatness of His plans for me, and how he was preparing me to lead this great nation."

CHAPTER 19

AN INCREDIBLE STORY

PERSEVERANCE

Joseph sighed as he continued, "So, there I was; now in prison. Even there, the God of my fathers blessed everything I did and before long, I was put in charge of all the prisoners. By now, the unseen presence became my best friend; my constant companion that I trusted without question. Whatever He told me to do, I did, no matter how crazy it appeared. Even though I was a slave and then a prisoner, I felt as if I was soaring as free as an eagle. It's as if I was on a great adventure with my unseen God. During that time, He kept reminding me of the dreams He had given me as a boy. Remember those dreams?" He asked, looking directly at his older brothers, as they bowed their heads in shame.

I knew that my God would release me from prison, but didn't know how or when. I had so many dreams during this time."

Then pulling his sons closer, he said, "There was one dream in which I had two sons. The first was named Manasseh, which means, 'God made me forget all my toil and all my father's house.' *(Genesis 41:51)*. The second son was named Ephraim, meaning 'For God has caused me to be fruitful in the land of my affliction.' *(Genesis 41:52)* I held on to that dream and believed that my God was preparing me for something beyond my imagination.

I even wrote a poem to them after the dream, because it was that day that my hope became more alive than ever. And on days when my circumstances made it difficult to believe, I read about you, my sons. Now here you are."

Joseph then pulled out a scroll and clearing his throat, said, "Let me read the poem that God used to maintain my sanity throughout those years:

"When Manasseh comes I will forget
the pain of the past
And the longing of what could be
The haunting memories of my father's house

would be gone at last
And the sun that shines today I will see.

When Manasseh comes my pain will
transform to purpose
In the light of the dawn each day
I will walk in the glow and strength of my affliction
And bask in freedom, now mine to stay.

When Manasseh comes my heart will be ready
To forgive and embrace every pain
My soul will always be at rest and peace
No matter how deep and crimson the stain.

Oh Manasseh! How my heart longs for you today
I know the joy you will bring in the fullness of time
As you prepare for Ephraim a perfect way
Bearing fruit that will be mine.

My hands stretch out for Ephraim
Whom I can see waiting in the wings
Manasseh, I will look for you in this season
Knowing that Ephraim will bring fruit,
purpose and reason.

My soul, my soul, why be downcast?
See Manasseh who will cause me
to forget my affliction
And Ephraim who will turn my thorns to roses
For all to see my pain was disguised as God's
perfectly planned purpose

Wait! Wait! My soul and let not your
heart be weary
My God is never hurried
He is forming Manasseh and Ephraim in
my innermost part
And in due season, He will bring them forth just as
He promised at the start."

There wasn't a dry eye in the room when he finished, including his own.

Pausing to regain composure, he continued, "I saw an opportunity when Pharaoh's butler and baker were thrown in prison. They each shared a dream and God gave me the interpretation. It happened just as God showed me. I asked them to appeal to Pharaoh on my behalf because I was wrongly imprisoned, but they didn't, and I remained in prison."

CHAPTER 20
AN INCREDIBLE STORY
PATIENCE

Taking a deep breath, Joseph continued, "My God continued to bless everything I did. And everyone was blessed, including the prisoners, after all, I was a prisoner myself. Two years later, the keeper of the prison called me and said that Pharaoh wanted to meet with me. I was shocked and excited because I knew this was my God appointed time to speak to Pharaoh, face to face, to plead my case. The guards gave me clean clothes and prepared me to meet him.

Imagine my surprise, when I stood before Pharaoh, all he wanted was for me to interpret his dreams. My unseen God gave the interpretation and I shared it with him. My God showed me that there was going to be seven years of plenty followed by seven years of famine. He then gave me a strategy to share with Pharaoh of how best to prepare for the famine. I assumed that

Potiphar and the keeper of the prison had already shared my history of success with them, because he made me second in command in the nation without question.

Even though it's a big job, I knew that God had prepared me when I was a slave and when I was in prison. You see, it was God's plan all along 'for such a time as this.' *(Esther 4:14)*

My deepest pain, however, was that I was separated from my family, especially my father, baby brother, and nephew. However, my unseen God's presence was so real, that I knew I was part of a great plan. But as much as I missed you, God told me that he would bring you to me. So, I waited, and waited. He has been so faithful to bring about everything and more He showed me in my dreams. I learned to trust Him.

There were times when waiting became unbearable. Even though I had it in my power to go to you, my God assured me that you would come. Imagine my amazement when you showed up the first time. I recognized you immediately. I can't say that it was my God who told me what to do, but I must admit that I enjoyed pretending not to be Joseph.

My desperate desire to see Benjamin almost gave me away. I had to keep one of you here to ensure that you would come back. After you left, I counted the days when I would see my baby brother. I wanted him to know that it was me, so I had my guards plant the one thing I knew he would recognize as belonging to our mother."

After he said this, he tenderly stroked Benjamin's hair, as tears began to well up in his eyes. Overcome with emotion, all the brothers wept and begged again for his forgiveness.

Leaning against Joseph, Benjamin said, "I recognized it immediately. But wondered how it could possibly have gotten in my sack because I had the cup under my cushion. Then the possibility that it was an exact replica hit me. There were too many coincidences and my heart filled with hope that you were my brother."

Joseph laughed, "I wanted you to know while trying to get you back with me. I hope you forgive me for planting the cup in your sack?"

Now crying uncontrollably, Benjamin said, "Oh brother, there is nothing to forgive. I wasn't afraid. I was hopeful."

Joseph said, "No more crying, this is a celebration. Remember, it's our God who brought me here for His purposes. God has given our fathers a great promise to make a nation of us, and this is part of His plan. We must trust His plan. Let's celebrate the God of our fathers, Abraham, Isaac and Israel, the God who keeps His promises."

CHAPTER 21
ONE NATION – ONE GOD

In the years proceeding Israel's death, his family multiplied. Joseph, Benjamin and Sychar bonded deeply as one family. With Joseph as the lord in the land, they were given the choicest property in Goshen, while their brothers received leftovers. Throughout their entire lives, they and their children prostrated themselves in homage to him. Seeing their dignity stripped before him, Sychar's passion to avenge his father's death waned. It was more than enough witnessing their humility and absolute dependence on Joseph.

Even though he had forgiven them, Joseph never allowed them to forget that he was lord of the land. They were required to prostrate themselves before him and come to him for everything. They lived out the rest of their lives in humiliation, dependence and surrender to their younger brother. In contrast, he showered Benjamin and Sychar with abundance.

Seeing this, their children began resenting Joseph, Benjamin, Sychar and their children. As the generations increased, the rift between them widened. Three generations later, Joseph took his last breath, after he made his family promise that they would bury his bones in the land God promised to give them.

God had blessed the Israelites immensely. They multiplied profusely and were successful in everything they did. So much so, that after the Pharaoh who knew Joseph died, the new king, who did not know Joseph, felt threatened. He said to his people, "Look, the people of the children of Israel are more and mightier than we; come, let us deal shrewdly with them, lest they multiply and it happen in the event of war, that they also join our enemies and fight against us, and so go up out of the land." *(Exodus 1:9)*

Afraid that they had become a nation in number themselves, the Egyptians enslaved the Israelites, including Joseph's descendants. They remained enslaved for approximately four hundred years. During which time, the rift between the brothers' descendants decreased.

For the first time they had the same heartbeat for their One God and one goal, their freedom. They, therefore, watched and waited for God to send a deliverer.

BOOK THREE

THE DESCENDENTS
OF
JACOB

CHAPTER 1

A TIME FOR EVERY SEASON

"It's time mother. We have to tell him now," she said urgently.

Aware of her daughter's impetuous and dramatic nature, her mother asked, "It's time for what?"

Mariam answered with an all-knowing air of a sage, "You know exactly who I'm referring to mother? He's older now and needs to know. I'm sure he knows he's one of us, but doesn't know his family or history."

Her mother, Jacohebed, looked up and said, "Oh, so you think so, do you? And how do you propose to tell him? You don't just walk up to a prince of Egypt and tell him you want to talk to him. This must be well planned my child. Your father and I have talked about it and we will let you know when we believe the time is right and how to make ourselves known to him."

"Mother, you know father barely has time to breathe these days. I say we don't delay; and besides, I have a plan," her daughter confidently retorted.

"You have another plan? You always have a plan, but I must admit, as crazy as your plans have been, they have worked out. Let's hear it," said her mother.

"Trust me mother," Mariam replied. "Remember, it was my idea to hide him when he was born and make a small ark and lay it in the river by Pharaoh's palace. I knew when Pharaoh's daughter would be there to make sure she saw it. And, I also made sure she hired you as his nursemaid, knowing she would need one for him. I was right about the timing then, and I'm right about it now. I know everything that goes on in that palace since I've been a slave there. Besides, I've been watching his routine and I know exactly when to talk to him."

Her mother nodded in affirmation and said, "You're right, my child. If it weren't for you, we wouldn't have him with us, even though he doesn't know his real family yet. What is your plan?"

Miriam's eyes lit up as she rambled, "He likes to walk through the gardens early in the morning. He seems to be a bit restless and likes to walk. It's more like pacing, though. Anyway, since I know his routine, I can take a short break from my cleaning chores. No one will miss me. I'm usually working on my own anyway. When he walks by, I can call his name and as soon as he turns around I'll just tell him that I'm his sister. Then I'll tell him about his family and invite...."

Interrupting her, Jacohebed said, "Is that your plan, to follow him as he's walking. What makes you think he's even interested in knowing who we are? And why do you think he will believe you. He is one of the princes of Egypt. He can have you killed and then kill us. He's one of them, Miriam, not one of us."

Dismissing all fears, Miriam, replied, "Oh, mother, you had similar concerns when I suggested putting him in the river, remember. You were concerned that no one would find him.

Then you were concerned that if they found him, that they would just kill him as they did the other baby boys. Remember all your objections? We must trust the God of our fathers as we did then. He must know who he is and who we are. God saved him for a purpose, who knows, it may be to deliver us from slavery and lead us to our own lands. Father has told us of God's promises to Abraham over and over. Well, perhaps this is part of God's plan for us."

"How did you ever become so fearless, my daughter? You may be right; however and whenever we tell him, we will be taking a risk, and if you want to, perhaps it's the right time. Let me talk to your father and brother first," her mother responded.

Gushing with self-confidence, Miriam said, "I know this plan will work mother. I'm feeling the same certainty as when he was born and I watched him float down the river to Pharaoh's daughter. The God of our fathers' is with us. Please talk to father and Aaron and let me know as soon as possible. I watch him every chance I get. Even though he looks like an Egyptian, I just know that he's one of us on the inside. He's my brother."

CHAPTER 2
A CRITICAL DECISION

Later that evening, Jochebed said to her husband and son, "Miriam thinks it's time again to tell Moses about us. She has a plan and isn't afraid to talk to him. What are your thoughts?"

Her husband, Amram said, "I think about him every day. I'm so proud of him and every time I see him in the field, I want to run to him and tell him that I'm his father. Then I remember that he's an Egyptian prince and I'm but a slave."

"He has turned out to be a fine young man," Aaron added. "He seems to have a tender heart. I hope his mother, I mean his adoptive mother, has told him that he's a Hebrew. But I'm sure he's wondering who his family is and why we put him in the river as a baby."

Affirming his wife, Amram said, "He is one of us. We took a chance to circumcise him, but I'm so glad we did. So, what's Miriam's plan. She works in the palace, and is the only one with access to him. Perhaps this is the right time. The worse that could happen is that he denies his heritage and turns against us."

Aaron said, "Let's not forget who we are, blood is thicker than water. I'm with Miriam, I think it's time. He will not deny his heritage."

Jochebed chimed in, "Miriam has been right in the past. It's because of God's wisdom in her that he's alive today. We trusted her then, we should trust her now. She's so excited to have him know that he's her brother. She has truly watched over him all these years."

Amram, tired from his day's work, said, "Then tell her to do as she believes God is leading. We're with her."

Aaron said, "Let me know when she plans to tell him. I'll tell the elders to seek the God of our fathers' favor. It's common knowledge among most of us that he's an Israelite anyway. They just don't know that he's my brother."

The following day, Miriam slipped away from the palace where she worked and lived. Finding her mother hanging clothes, she ran up to her and asked, "Well, mother, did you talk to father and Aaron? What did they say? Can I tell Moses? I can't wait."

Turning around, her mother said, "Greetings daughter, I trust you had a good day and night. And, yes, I spoke to your father and brother. The answer is 'yes,' we agree that it's time to let him know. Can you tell him tomorrow as Aaron wanted to talk to the elders first and offer prayers to the God of our fathers?"

Jumping with delight, Miriam, kissed her mother on the cheek and said, "I knew it. I knew it. This is God. I can't wait to talk to him. I'll do it tomorrow morning. I'm sure as soon as I tell him, that he'll want to meet his family, so don't be surprised if he comes here. I'll try to arrange to bring him here as soon as possible. It's going to be okay, mother, I know that our God is with us in this."

CHAPTER 3
THE RECURRING DREAM

No one slept the following night. Aaron
and the elders stayed awake crying out for God's
favor and protection. Amram, Jochebed and
Miriam did the same.

As they prayed, later that night, thirty-five-
year old, Moses had one of his reality-like
recurring dreams since he was twenty. In the
dream, he *had accidently broken off a twig from a
dry, dead bush. Picking it up from the ground, he
looked at the broken branch in his hands, and was
stunned to see it sprouting leaves. He stared at
the twig in wonder and unbelief, yet he couldn't
deny what he saw. Feeling afraid of holding this
living, growing stick, he flung it in the air. It
floated upward and disappeared into the clouds.
Moses stared upward as it floated away. Then as
if returning from nowhere, the twig floated down
and reattached itself to the dead bush. The bush
grew and kept on growing until it became a*

gigantic, blooming tree, loaded with different kinds of low hanging fruit.

As if jolted, he awoke with the same fright as he always did following this dream. It was usually at the same point in the dream, with the broken, dead branch coming to life and spreading into a massive tree. His heart raced with overwhelming fear as he sat up in bed, again in a cold sweat. He asked the same question of his Egyptian gods, "What manner of dream is this?"

Awaking the following morning with the dream swirling in his mind, he prepared to go for his usual stroll. Today of all days, he needed to walk and think. Believing there was a message and purpose for that recurring dream, he couldn't wait to search it out ~ again.

No sooner did he begin on his regular walking path, that he heard a female voice call out from the bushes, "My lord, my lord, I have something important to share with you?"

Looking around and seeing no one, he shook his head and continued walking. He heard the same voice again, this time there was a rustle in the bushes. He stopped and asked, "Who's there, show yourself."

A short, rounded figure emerged, bowing before him as she did. Moses asked, "Who are you? You look very familiar? Are you one of our household slaves?"

Bowing before him again, she raised her head, and said, "Yes, my lord. I am one of your humble slaves."

When she raised her head, Moses was shocked to see his eyes staring back at him. She looked to be at least ten years his senior, with long, black, wavy hair. Not only did her eyes seem familiar, but her nose did as well. He thought, *There is something different about her. I can't wait to hear what she has to say.*

Discerning that she was somewhat afraid from the tremor in her voice, he put her at ease, saying, "Don't be afraid, daughter. Speak, I'm curious about what you have to say. Are you an Israelite?"

She bowed again, and said, "Yes, I am an Israelite, of the tribe of Levi, who was a brother of the Egyptian governor, named Joseph. I'm sure you have heard of him. He is a legend among our people. A long time ago, he saved Egypt and our family from famine."

Intrigued as to where this conversation was leading, he replied, "Yes, he is well known in our history, among the Pharaohs. I'm very well acquainted with Joseph's accomplishments in Egypt but didn't know he was a Hebrew."

Feeling more relaxed, Miriam asked, "Sir, do you know your personal history?"

Moses looked at her inquisitively and said, "Because you're asking, it appears that you may know my history better than I do. I know that I was named Moses by my mother because she pulled me out of the river. She also told me that I'm an Israelite and I'm circumcised. None of the other Egyptians are circumcised. That's all I know. As to how I got in the river or why, I don't know. If you know, please share as these questions have plagued me all my life."

Miriam exhaled and blurted out, "I know. I'm your older sister who put you in the river to save your life. I have watched over you since then. You are as I am, from the tribe of Levi, son of Jacob, Isaac and Abraham. Your mother and father are still alive; and you have a brother, named Aaron. They would like to meet you."

Moses said, "Slow down. How do I know you're telling me the truth? My mother kept the basket as a reminder of the day that I floated towards her. If you describe it, I'll know you're telling the truth."

Miriam smiled, reflecting on the past, she said, "I see it even now, vividly, because my father, brother and I made it. It was oval." Then cupping her arms into an oval shape, she continued, "We covered it with papyrus and overlaid it with asphalt and pitch. Mother wrapped you in a thick brown cloth. We all held you close and placed you on the river at the right time, knowing that the God of our fathers would guide you to Pharaoh's daughter."

Moses' eyes filled with tears as Miriam described the basket he saw almost daily, growing up in the palace. As the tears rolled down his face, he stared at her and said, "My sister, my sister. How I longed for my family. My mother couldn't share any information about who they were. She assured me, however, that they must have loved me very much to go to such lengths to save my life. When can I meet the rest of my family?"

Miriam, whose character was to speak first and think later, declared, "How about this evening. I'll take you to them. I'd take you now, but father and Aaron will be out at the worksite. Mother is at home though, we can go and meet her now. But I must return to my chores or I'll be missed, so let's make it tonight then. Meet me here and I'll take you."

They hugged each other, and Moses said, "I can't wait until tonight. I'll meet you here then. In the meantime, let's not make our relationship public, I don't want any harm to come to you and the family, nor to me. I also want to talk to my mother, my adoptive mother."

Miriam nodded in agreement, bowed before him and walked away.

CHAPTER 4
A MOTHER'S HEART

It was one of the longest days of their lives. Moses continued walking, while processing the conversation he just had. His head swimming with questions, he thought, *I'm related to the great Governor, Joseph, the Israelite. They must have left that part out in my history lessons as every reference and depiction of him was as an Egyptian. I'm going to meet my parents tonight. What shall I say to them? What do they think of me? They are slaves and I'm a prince. How do I relate to them? How can I help them?*

Deep in thought, he didn't see his mother, Bithiah, approaching in the opposite direction with her entourage. As she neared him, she said, "Moses, just the person I wanted to see today. My favorite, unmarried son, how are you?"

Moses shifted to the present, bent over and kissed his mother's hand. He said, "Always good to see you mother. And your only son, your only

unmarried son, is well. Can we talk in private?
There's something I need to share with you."

Bithiah said, "I trust it's good news.
You've chosen a wife. I can't wait to hear who it
is and we can begin planning your wedding
celebration."

Moses laughed and said, "Not so fast
mother. I haven't chosen a wife yet, you know my
concerns, besides, I haven't found anyone who
will accept me."

"Any woman will be delighted to be my
handsome, son's wife," his mother said proudly.

Changing the subject, Moses replied, "Well,
after what I have to share, we may have to shift
perspectives. When can we chat?"

Looking concerned, his mother said, "This
is urgent. Let's have lunch. We haven't had
lunch together in a long time. Come to my
quarters and it'll be just the two of us. I look
forward to seeing you."

Moses kissed her hands again and said,
"See you then mother. And please don't arrange
any more meetings with potential wives for me.
Promise?"

His mother winked and said, "I can't promise that my son. It's a mother's duty to see her son married. You're over thirty now. You should have been married years ago. Okay, I'll drop the subject, for now, if you insist. See you later, son."

Within a few hours, Moses and his mother met privately in her quarters. He related the experience he had earlier that morning with his sister and shared that he was going to meet his birth parents later that evening. With no small amount of concern, Bithiah, asked, "Are you sure she is your sister?"

Moses replied, "Yes, I'm sure. She described my basket perfectly. She said that she, her father and brother made it as they prayed that the God of their fathers would guide me to you."

Bithiah's eyes misted as she replied, "I know that you were sent to me. It's as if a Divine hand guided you into my arms. And the moment I saw you, I knew you were mine. You were the most adorable baby I'd ever seen. I loved you at first glance and love you even more today. You have been the perfect son to me."

"Mother," said Moses, "I'm meeting my birth parents tonight and I have so many questions. I'm actually somewhat nervous about meeting them."

"Son, there is no need to be nervous. I always knew that they must have loved you to put you in the river. They also trusted in their God to guide you to me. I've had you all these years and I don't object to sharing you with others. In fact, I would like to meet these remarkable people as well," his mother replied.

Moses responded, "I am so blessed to have you as my mother. Meeting them will help me put the pieces of the mosaics of my life in focus. I'll finally know who I am and not waver between two worlds."

"But you know who you are. You are my son, the daughter of Pharaoh's son, a prince of Egypt. All I know is that the gods sent you to me for a purpose, and I've been waiting to see that purpose unfold," his mother stated affectionately.

"Perhaps I'll get more insight tonight, mother," said Moses. "Now do you understand why I haven't married. I don't believe an Egyptian woman would want me, and I can't marry from my own people. At least not now."

"Oh son," declared his mother, in her most affectionate tone, "I understand you better than you think. And always remember that I want the best for you, no matter what, or how it will impact me. Let me know how things go after your meeting tonight, no matter what time you finish. Promise?"

Affirming his mother's wishes, Moses kissed her on the cheek and then asked, "I have a huge favor to ask."

"Just name it my son, if it's in my powers to give, it's yours," replied his mother.

Moses asked, "I would like to take a present to my birth family tonight. I know you treasure the floating carrier you found me in, but I would like to give it back to them. I think it will be a fitting gift, that I return it to them. I can't imagine how much they suffered all these years, knowing who I was, but unable to share who they were to me. It will be symbolic of my re-entry to their lives."

His mother responded, "If that's what you want my son, please take it. It's yours and theirs. It's your heart I'm after, and I think I already have it. It's brought me so many happy moments since you came into my arms, I hope it will bring them many happy moments as well. I can only imagine how difficult their lives are." Reaching for the carrier and then filling it with fruits and other delicacies, she said, "Here, take these to them as well. Please let them know it's from me."

Unable to control his tears, he hugged her and said, "Thank you mother. This means more to me than you will ever know. By the way, I have a sister who has been one of our household slaves before I was born."

Bithiah immediately responded, "I would love to meet her. Bring her to me sometime. I will add her to my household staff and show her much kindness because she's your sister."

Giving his mother another hug, Moses thanked her again for everything and left. The restlessness he had experienced most of his adult life was now surprisingly missing.

CHAPTER 5
IDENTITY RESTORED

With none of the Egyptian makeup and princely trappings, Miriam hardly recognized her brother. When she saw the basket in his hands filled with food, she grabbed hold of his arm, and said, "I am so glad you're my brother. Let's go, there is much to discuss."

Walking with his head down so as not to be recognized, Moses and Miriam reached her home. It was a very small hut, built with wood and straw, covered with straw and animal skins. The entrance was rectangular, with a narrow entrance, and the floor was clay, that was swept clean. The furnishings were meager; a few straw mats scattered randomly on the floor; large carrier jugs stood against the walls; several baskets gathered in one corner; and there was a wood like tray containing cups and plates.

Anticipating Moses' visit, his mother nervously paced their small living space, while his father and brother, stood silently, gazing out the front door. They first heard Miriam's saying, "We're almost there." And in seconds, they were at the door. They saw a taller and fatter than the average Israelite, bowing his head, to enter the narrow space.

A long pregnant silence filled the room as he stared at his mother, father and brother. Recognizing that these were the most important people he will ever meet, Moses, being a humble man, bowed before them in reverence.

Miriam was the first to break the silence, "Well, I told you everything would be fine. Look, mother, look at what's in his arms."

With tears streaming from his eyes, and trying to regain composure, Moses said, "I brought you something. The fruit and other delicacies are from my mother. She sends her warmest greetings."

His mother, who looked like an older version to her daughter, Miriam, not knowing what to do or say, bowed before him and said, "Thank you."

Moses said, "Please don't bow before me. It is I who should bow before you, mother and father." And looking at Aaron, he reached out his hands and said, "Brother. I have wanted to know my true family all these years. Now I find that you were living less than ten miles away from me. Is this where I was born?"

Catching her breath, his mother began touching his face and answered, "Yes, my son, this is where you were born. What a handsome face. You were such a beautiful child. I knew you would grow up to be a handsome man."

His father approached and said, "Son, I've waited thirty-five years for this moment. Welcome home. Yes, I see that you are indeed my very handsome son."

Finding his voice, Aaron exclaimed, "My baby brother has come home. It's so good to see you here. I've seen you riding with the royal chariots and on occasion, have glimpsed you surveying the worksites. Now you're here, welcome."

Not quite knowing what else to say, an awkward silence permeated the room. Miriam broke the silence and said in their native tongue, as they had been speaking in Egyptian before, "I told you he is kind and compassion and would love us."

Moses, who didn't understand their dialect looked around and said, "I'm afraid I don't understand your language. I was educated in everything Egyptian and it's a disgrace to speak the language of our slaves."

His father said, "Oh, we will have to teach you our language. We all speak Egyptian as well, your Pharaoh mandates it, but we speak our own language when we're together."

"I'd like that," Moses, responded. "I want to know everything there is to know about my family."

"But first we want to know everything about you," Aaron said. "Miriam has been watching you ever since you were brought to the palace, so we know a little about you through her."

Moses cleared his throat and asked rhetorically, "Where do I begin?"

CHAPTER 6
HIS STORY

Beginning when he first became aware that he was not an Egyptian, but an Israelite, Moses said, "I remember the day clearly. I must have been five or six then. Mother and I were walking together in the garden, when I heard someone whisper, 'He looks just like the other slaves. Yet here he is, walking as if he's a prince.' Mother heard it also. Since I was the only boy walking with my mother's entourage, I knew they were talking about me. She squeezed my hand and continued ignoring the comment.

When we returned to her quarters, she said, 'I have something to share with you, my son. I planned to tell you when you were a bit older, but it's time.'" Moses paused and pointed to the basket, and then continued, "It was then she showed me the basket and told me that I floated out of nowhere on the river into her arms. She believed the gods had sent me to her because she longed for a son. She also shared that I was the son of one of the Hebrew slaves, who loved me very much, and wanted to spare my life from her father's wrath. From that time forward, I longed to know my birth family."

With tears beginning to swell in his eyes, he continued, "Mother guarded me and made sure that I was treated as a true prince in the palace. There was no external distinction between me and the other princes. The gods gave me great success in our battles and protected me. God has especially gifted me with administration. I manage all the resources of Egypt. Nothing is bought or sold without my consent. I've achieved great success and victories in battle, but there was something missing. Even though I tried very hard, I couldn't identify myself as an Egyptian. Now I know what the missing pieces were, you, my family, my history. You are my identity and I want to learn everything about you."

His mother stroked his face again, as his father patted him on the back and said, "We have been praying for you, my son. Not a day passed without thinking of you. We have been looking forward to this day for a long time, but were afraid to approach you. You are after all a prince and we are slaves."

His mother asked, "You never married. You're thirty-five years old. Why haven't you married by now? You are such a handsome son. I know just the woman for you."

Embarrassed, Aaron said, "Mother, now is not the time to discuss this."

Miriam, who was unusually quiet, chimed in and said, "Mother, I think I know who you have a mind. She would make him a perfect wife."

Laughing, Moses said, "Now it seems that I have three mothers. How could I marry when I've felt so incomplete? It's as if, I was leading a double life, being a Hebrew, but living as an Egyptian. Enough about me, I want to know about you, our family, everything."

CHAPTER 7
THEIR STORY

His father, Amram, together with his brother, Aaron, shared their story. They began by re-telling the stories they learned from prior generations. Then, beginning with God's covenant with Abraham, the first Hebrew, his father shared, "It began with a choice our patriarch, Abraham made. His father, Terah, wanted to leave Ur and settle in Canaan. He took Abraham with him, but he died along the way, and they ended up settling in Haran. It was here where Abraham first heard the voice of an unseen God. The voice told him to leave Haran and go to a place where He would lead him. That if he did, this God would make him into a great nation and he and his descendants would be a blessing to the world. This was intriguing to him, because he and his wife, Sarah, were already older and she was barren.

Abraham was mesmerized with the voice of this unseen God and followed Him without question. After wandering from place to place, he settled in Canaan but his wife, was still barren. Throughout this time, the voice of his God assured him that he and Sarah would have a child and that his descendants would be great in the world. You see, they were getting up there in age, (they were in their nineties), when an angel of God appeared to him and told him that they would have a son in a year. As you can imagine, they both laughed, but nonetheless they believed what God had promised."

"A child in their nineties?" Moses posed in disbelief. "I imagine that would be hard to believe."

"It was then that God made a covenant with him and said, 'This is My covenant which you shall keep, between Me and you and your descendants after you: Every male child among you shall be circumcised; and you shall be circumcised in the flesh of your foreskins, and it shall be a sign of the covenant between Me and you. He who is eight days old among you shall be circumcised, every male child in your generations, he who is born in your house or bought with money from any foreigner who is not your descendant...The covenant shall be in your flesh for an everlasting covenant.'" *(Genesis17: 10 – 13)*

Amram continued, "I can't imagine being circumcised as an adult, much less close to a hundred years old, but Abraham obeyed God and did what He asked. It was shortly after this, that his old, barren wife, conceived and had Isaac. Every descendent of Abraham, through Isaac, has been circumcised at eight days old, including you, my son. Circumcision is our external sign of our commitment to be God's chosen people, and essential to our faith."

Aaron then expounded on their ancestors' experiences with God beginning with Jacob, who was renamed Israel; and his twelve sons who were called Israelites. He then shared Joseph's story and how they came to Egypt and live in Goshen and how long they had been slaves.

Recognizing a pause, Moses asked, "I've had plenty of interaction with Ishmaelite slave traders and I know they also claim to be descendants from Abraham and an Egyptian, named Hagar. I believe it's the same Abraham you mentioned, but I've never heard of Isaac or Jacob. I now know that Jacob is the father of the Israelites, but who was Isaac? Did he father a nation named after him, like Ishmael?"

His father answered, "That is true. Abraham is also the father of Ishmael. His mother was an Egyptian and she gave birth to Ishmael because Abraham's wife, Sarah was barren. Since she never had a child, and was old, beyond child bearing age, they thought God's solution was for them to have a child through surrogacy, by natural means. But God had a different plan all along.

He had promised Abraham that he would have a son through Sarah as a sign of His covenant. The sign had to come through spiritual means from God and not by natural means of man. They finally had a child when they were in their nineties. This was an amazing miracle for Sarah because she was well pass child bearing age at the time she became pregnant. God planned it that way so that there would be no question that his birth was anything but a spiritual sign from heaven.

Isaac, therefore, was the sign of the promise that God would raise up a nation of people for Himself through Abraham and Sarah. Because he was the sign of God's promise, he didn't father a tribe. But his son, Jacob did. He had twelve sons. We refer to them as the twelve tribes of Israel: Reuben was the first-born son, then Simeon, Levi, Judah, Dan, Naphtali, Gad, Asher, Issachar, Zebulun, Joseph, and Benjamin. We are from the tribe of Levi."

Then to everyone's surprise, Miriam exclaimed, "We sing a song about our Isaac, as our sign of deliverance." And without hesitation, she began singing:

When our Isaac comes
Our grief and sorrow will be gone
When God shifts our times and seasons
We will no longer doubt but will have reason
To shout to any who will listen

That God and God only can break through any
prison.

When our Isaac comes
Our mourning will turn to dancing
And the trial of waiting will end with singing
The God of our fathers will exchange our fears and
weakness
Into an eternal festival with no more shadows or
darkness.

When our Isaac comes
Oh! The waiting will be more precious than gold
With new life laughing in our soul
To finally hold our Isaac in our hearts
Will be beyond any earthly imagination or charms.

When our Isaac comes
All shadows will disappear
As His face we will see so clear
When our Isaac comes
He will give us feet to run on high places
To be as free as a bird in all life stages
When our Isaac comes

When our Isaac comes
When our Isaac comes
We will be free
When our Isaac comes.

CHAPTER 8

QUESTIONS AND CLARIFICATION

Moses asked incredulously, "One other question, this Joseph that you mentioned, who was the governor of Egypt, was he Hebrew? I've learned all Egyptian history. I know of Joseph as a great Egyptian governor who saved the nation from famine and expanded our territory, but I never knew he was an Israelite. He was always represented as an Egyptian."

Aaron chimed in, and sounding a bit annoyed, retorted, "I'm not surprised. I'm sure the Egyptians don't want to be reminded that one of their greatest leaders, was an Israelite. He was not only a Hebrew, but our relative. He and our patriarch, Levi were brothers, sons of one father, Jacob. He refused to be buried as an Egyptian. In fact, we have his bones as his last request was that we were to bury him in the promise land. You see, he believed that one day, we would be our own nation, just as our God promised."

Continuing, Aaron added, "We hope to bury him in our land soon. We know we're not going to be slaves forever, because of the promises God made to our forefathers to give us our own land. We will have our own nation one day; a land flowing with milk and honey. Each generation has been tracking the cycle of the moon and we know the time is drawing near for our release. There are at least two elders from each of the twelve tribe. I'm one of the elders for the tribe of Levi."

Jochebed chimed in, "You're overwhelming him with too much information. We're not going anywhere soon, and hopefully we'll see you again."

"Yes, now that I've found you, I'll visit often," Moses shared. "I especially want to learn your language, after all, I'm one of you. And I want to know about my family." He then asked, "Aaron, can you teach me?"

Miriam piped up and said, "I can teach you. We can meet as often as you like in the palace and I'll teach you our language and anything else you like."

Aaron interjected, "She's right. With the hard labor we do, there isn't much time for anything else except sleep when we get home. But I'd like to introduce you to the elders when you're available. There's a reason why you're in Pharaoh's palace. Perhaps you can negotiate our release along with the elders."

Moses, who was more of a listener than a speaker said, "I'd like that."

They ate together, made plans for their next meeting, and said a happy, yet tearful goodbye. He and Miriam then returned to the palace.

CHAPTER 9
HIS SISTER'S INSIGHTS

Moses' head was swimming with information as he walked back with Miriam. He tried processing it all, but Miriam chatted, barely pausing long enough for a breath. Half listening, he commented, "I knew about Joseph, but didn't know my rich history. Thanks for filling in the blanks."

Miriam proudly retorted, "I know our God is going to get us out of here soon. I can feel it and believe you are part of his plan for our release. I've always thought so. He promised to send us a deliverer and we know he must identify with us, be one with us, but not be a slave like us. We need someone who doesn't have the mindset of a slave like we do. Someone who understands the Egyptian way of thinking, who knows how to lead and is familiar with Pharaoh's court. That's you, brother. I believe our God saved you out of the river to be our deliverer."

Moses jumped in and said, "He should also know your God, don't you think? And that I don't know. I know all the Egyptian gods, but have never heard of the God of our fathers. I may not be your deliverer after all, sister."

Ignoring his statement and pausing for a quick breath, she continued, "And when we leave, we're taking Joseph's bones with us. That was his last wish; to take his bones to our promised land. We get to see it about four times a year as a reminder that one day we're leaving. No matter how discouraging it gets, we have hope whenever we see his bones and remember his words. I'll take you to see them sometime. When would you like to start learning our language? It's easy and I know you'll pick it up in no time."

Trying to keep up with her communication, Moses responded to her last question and answered, "We can start now, if you like. We still have a couple of miles ahead. And before I forget, my mother, my adoptive mother, wants to meet you. She wants to show you favor and give you a position inside her court. Would you like that?"

Miriam let out a low squeal of excitement, "Yes, I would love that. No more cleaning up after the other slaves. I can't believe that I've been doing that for all these years. Won't they be envious when they see me elevated to work in Pharaoh's daughter's court. You are special brother. I knew it, I said you were special when you were born. Now here we are, and I'm getting a promotion. Thank you, please tell your adoptive mother I can't wait to meet her and start working in her quarters. I'll be the best worker she ever had. She'll never regret it. But of course, I won't be there long, because we're all leaving. God is taking us out from this place. I can feel it."

With his head drowning with information, Moses quietly said, "Yes, I believe He is too."

CHAPTER 10
THE RECURRING DREAM

When Moses returned to the palace, he went immediately to his mother's suite. She was eager to see him and greeted him, saying, "I waited up to see you and can't wait to hear what your family is like."

Yawning, Moses said, "I can tell you this mother, my birth mother is just like you. She wanted to know why I haven't married yet, and suggested someone she knows to be the perfect wife for me. My sister, Miriam, said the same. Now I not only have one mother, I have three."

Bithiah laughed and said, "Well, it's because they recognize that you are a fine, handsome man who needs a wife and have plenty children. How is your father and brother?"

"Mother," said Moses, "I've found the missing piece to who I am. I'm so thankful that God brought me to you and to have you for a mother. You know I've always felt incomplete.

Today, for the first time, I know who I am. I know my identity but there's so much more to learn. I'm a Hebrew, mother, not an Egyptian. If it's okay with you, I no longer want to dress like an Egyptian. I'm just Moses, an Israelite."

Bithiah paused, deeply thinking through what her son just shared, and said, "Son, why don't you think it through before you make any decisions. You've just learned a great deal of information about who you are, your family history and so much more. Let it all sink in before acting."

"That's sage advice, mother," Moses replied. "I'm tired and know you are as well. Let's get some sleep and I'll see you in the morning. Perhaps we can talk more then."

Kissing each other goodnight, Moses left and went to his quarters. Before nodding off, he said to himself, *I need to know this God of my fathers.* Later that night, he had a similar dream to the one he had intermittently over the last twelve years. *In this dream the dead bush was burning but not being consumed. He stared at it until the flames died down, then he broke off one*

of the burned twigs and flung it into the air. The
twig floated up and disappeared. It then
reappeared and reattached itself to the dry, dead
bush, that began growing, sprouting leaves and
flowers and producing a variety of fruit.

He awoke with a jolt, as he had in the past.
This time, he spoke to the God of his fathers,
Abraham, Isaac and Jacob, and asked, "What is
the meaning of this dream?"

CHAPTER 11

INTERPRETING THE SIGNS

Deciding it was in his best interest, and the best interest of the Israelites, not to publicly unveil his Hebrew heritage, Moses continued as before. He, however, immersed himself in learning his history, language, culture, family and people. Believing it was time for his brother to meet with the tribal leaders, Aaron invited him to one of their meetings.

On the night of the meeting, Aaron handed him a mat and said, "You'll need this where we're going."

"Where are we going?" Asked Moses.

"We're going to the elders meeting place," responded Aaron. "Only those who are invited know the way. This secret place was built by the first elders and it's where we pray, record our history and discuss our freedom. Come, the other elders are excited to meet you."

Moses followed Aaron into a small hut with a tiny entrance. He then walked into a back room, where he moved four large flat stones that uncovered an opening. They stepped down several steps before coming to the bottom. They then walked through a narrow, winding passage, before entering a large, open space. Moses observed approximately twenty men sitting on their mats, in silence.

Whispering, he asked Aaron, "Why are they silent?"

"We believe that our God will speak to us as He spoke to our forefathers," Aaron whispered. "When we come into this special place, we remain silent before Him; waiting to hear His voice. He has not spoken yet, but we know He will, so we wait a while in silence before we begin our meeting."

Moses nodded in fascination, as his experience with the Egyptian gods, (not including the current Pharaoh) was the exact opposite; the louder and more boisterous the people became, the more they believed they heard from their gods.

Moses placed his mat next to Aaron's, and they joined the group in silence. Three other elders joined and within a short time, one elder cleared his throat as a signal to begin the meeting. He said, "We thank the God of our fathers for His presence, wisdom and favor towards us." Then turning to Moses, he said, "We're delighted that you can join us. Aaron has told us much about you and we have seen your compassion to our people."

Moses replied, "I wish I could do more than show compassion."

The elder then introduced himself, and everyone in the room. Another elder stood up, and walking to the wall, said, "The time is drawing near. God's word to our forefather, Abraham, was that we would be in captivity for approximately four hundred years. According to this word, we will be freed in our generation. God will give us the strategy and one of us here may lead us out."

Turning to Moses, another elder said, "Moses, I believe you are God's chosen leader. It's no accident that you are with us today. Just as

God raised up Joseph, a Hebrew, as a great leader in Egypt to save us from the famine, so I believe He is raising you up, another leader in Egypt, and a Hebrew, to deliver us."

Another elder said, "I disagree, why would God raise up an outsider, even though he is an Israelite, to deliver us. We are all qualified candidates."

"Given the hard labor we've been subjected to, our people are suspicious of all leaders. God may have another plan altogether," commented another elder.

This debate continued for some time, until Aaron interjected. With his commanding voice, he said, "Elders, let's stop this bickering. Our concern should not be about who God will raise up to deliver us, but that He will deliver us. I don't know about you, but as long as I know, without any doubt, that God is with our leader, then I'm on his side. I believe that God has chosen my brother for this task. Who here knows the palace and the Egyptian ways? Who here has direct access to Pharaoh? Who here has lead great armies to victory? Who here has managed

the affairs of a nation?" Silence engulfed the room as he spoke. "I believe God saved my brother from the river 'for such a time as this.'"
(Esther 4:4)

An elder from the tribe of Judah stood up and said, "I agree with our brother Aaron. God Himself, shall raise up His deliverer for us."

Moses listened.

CHAPTER 12
TAKING ACTION

Now approaching his fortieth birthday, Moses felt like a disappointment and failure. The more the elders looked to him as God's deliverer for His people, the more he shrank in the shadows. Torn between two worlds, he felt paralyzed in both. With his frustration mounting over his helplessness to rescue his people, he cried out to the God of his fathers, "If you are real, as they say you are, then why don't you do something!"

One day, during a routine survey of the slave labor camp, as he had seen thousands of times before, "he saw an Egyptian beating a Hebrew, one of his brethren." *(Exodus 2:11)* Out of frustration, anger, and compassion, he reacted. Then looking around to ensure he would not be seen, "he killed the Egyptian and hid him in the sand." *(Exodus 2:12)*

The following day, during a similar routine survey, he saw two Hebrew men fighting, and he said to the one who did the wrong, "Why are you striking your companion?"

Then he [the Israelite] said, "Who made you a prince and a judge over us? Do you intend to kill me as you killed the Egyptian?" *(Exodus 2:13)*

Realizing that his secret was exposed, and feeling like a man without a country, neither belonging to Egypt nor Israel, he panicked and said, [to himself] *Surely this thing is known!* *(Exodus 2:14)*

Moses wasted no time. He returned to the palace, said a tearful goodbye to his mother, and under the cover of darkness, went to say goodbye to his birth family. Aaron, who was already aware that he had killed an Egyptian, asked, "My brother, what made you take such drastic action. Surely you have seen other Israelites beaten, and some even killed by the Egyptian slave masters."

Breathlessly, Moses replied, "I don't know what came over me. Since the God of our fathers has not acted, I felt that I had to something. Why is He allowing His people to suffer? Surely, this

God has power to deliver His people with or without a deliverer. This must come to an end. Now I'm running for my life because I know Pharaoh will learn of my actions soon, and my life is worth nothing. Forget about me brother. I'm so sorry to disappoint all of you." Then, kissing his parents, and hugging his brother and sister, the Egyptian Prince fled into the night; and ran into God's graduate school for kingdom leadership.

CHAPTER 13

THE NEXT FORTY YEARS

Already familiar with the territory surrounding Egypt's borders, Moses decided to head to Midian. Knowing that Pharaoh's army would not pursue him into the vast desert, he began his trek. Not taking any chances, he travelled under the cover of night and slept in caves by day. After running and walking the first two days, he finally decided to rest. Finding a safe location, he laid down from sheer exhaustion. With his mind in turmoil over his dilemma, he fell asleep. No sooner had he fallen asleep, when the recurring dream invaded his rest. In this dream however, *when he picked up the dry twig, it crumbled in his hands and turned to ashes. Then scattering the ashes in the air, he was stunned to see it floating upward, then returning to the dead bush, that revived and began blooming.*

Awakening with a fright, he said, "Everything I've touched since I learned about the God of my fathers have turned to ashes. He obviously does not need me, if He even exists. Therefore, I no longer need Him. I am not only without a country, but also without a God. What then is the purpose of my life?"

Overcome with self-pity, he continued moving forward. During the empty, dark days of traveling, he reflected on his life, especially the last five years. He pondered on what he could have done differently and everything wrong with his life. His thoughts always lead him to one conclusion, he was worthless, purposeless, a dismal failure and outcast. His only hope was to settle into a new life in Midian where he was not known. He therefore continued moving forward.

Finally reaching Midian, he sat at a well, not knowing what to do next. As he sat exhausted, seven women came to the well to water their flock. Other shepherds then came harassing the women and attempted to drive them away. Observing this, his righteous anger to rescue the defenseless, rose up. In an instant, the confident, courageous, warrior, former prince of Egypt, jumped to their rescue and drove the shepherds away.

Having fled in haste, Moses had not removed or changed his Egyptian attire or makeup. The women, therefore, thought he was an Egyptian and ran home to tell their father, "An Egyptian delivered us from the hand of the shepherds, and he also drew enough water for us and watered the flock." *(Exodus 2:19)* Wanting to thank the Egyptian stranger, their father, Jethro, invited him to share a meal. Moses stayed with Jethro as a shepherd for his flock for the next forty years.

CHAPTER 14
THE RELUCTANT DELIVERER

During the ensuing years, Moses married one of Jethro's daughters and became a shepherd. Forgetting the life of the past, and with no vision of a future, he existed one day at a time. The highlight of his life, was when his wife, Zipporah, bore a son and he named him "Gershom, for he said, "I have been a stranger in a foreign land." *(Exodus 2:22)*. Knowing that circumcision was the sign of the covenant with the God of his fathers, he chose not to circumcise him. For he said, "I am a man without God or country."

During the first ten of those years, he walked and talked to his sheep. Occasionally, he would look up and cry out to the unseen and nameless God of his ancestors. However, there was silence in return. Gradually, over the next three decades, he stopped looking up, stopped believing, and gave no thought of this unseen, nameless God of his fathers or any other god. Such was the life that Moses settled into for the next forty years.

Within a short time, he developed a routine of leading his flock to green pastures and water. As he did, he learned humility in putting the needs of his sheep before his own. Within a short time, he named each sheep and became intimately familiar with their behavior, so much so, that he anticipated their every action. He watched over them and protected them with his life. He ate when they ate, walked when they walked, talked to them, sang over them, rested when they rested, drank water when they drank water, and slept when they slept.

He rejoiced with every birth and grieved every loss. He went after each wondering stray and disciplined them with his staff to ensure they did not wonder off again. Then, pressing the stray close to his heart, he allowed it to feel his heartbeat, knowing that the sheep would remain close to him from that day forward.

Moses' joy and delight each day, was leading them to safety, food, water and rest. They in turn, knew his voice and responded to his call. They depended on him for everything and waited on him, trusting him to provide all their needs. Moses was finally content with his life in his safe, secure, predictable world. After forty years in the desert with his sheep, he not only knew what it was like to be a sheep, but he also knew how to lead them.

Never questioning his life, he quietly and humbly surrendered all visions and dreams and never had that recurring dream again. He simply accepted his life, and destiny, as a shepherd.

Then, on a day like any other, on the heels of his eightieth birthday, Moses led his sheep "to the back of the desert and came to [the mountain of] Horeb." *(Exodus 3:1)* To his amazement, he saw a flickering, bright light ahead. He cautiously approached the light, leaving his sheep at a safe distance behind. Having passed this bush hundreds of times over the last forty years, he was mesmerized by the fiery light. As he drew nearer to see this unbelievable sight, a voice coming from the fire called his name, "Moses, Moses." *(Exodus 3:4)*

Not knowing who was calling, Moses automatically answered, "Here I am." *(Exodus 3:4)*

The compelling voice then said, "Take your sandals off your feet for the place where you stand is holy ground." The voice continued, "I am the God of your father – the God of Abraham, the God of Isaac, and the God of Jacob." *(Exodus 3:5)*

Knowing the thoughts and questions he had in his heart toward the God of his fathers, and seeing the miraculous light before him, "Moses hid his face, for he was afraid to look upon God." *(Exodus 3:6)*

Ignoring Moses' response, God came straight to the point and told him that He has seen and heard the cries "of My people who are in Egypt." *(Exodus 3:7)* God further shared that He "came down to deliver them out of the hand of the Egyptians, and to bring them up from that land to a good and large land, to a land flowing with milk and honey…" *(Exodus 3:8)*

God said, "I will send you to Pharaoh that you may bring My people, the children of Israel, out of Egypt." *(Exodus 3:10)*

Stripped of all confidence of himself and this unseen, unnamed God, Moses responded, "Who am I that I should go to Pharaoh, and that I should bring the children of Israel out of Egypt?" *(Exodus 3:11)*

Ignoring his objections once again, God assured him that, "He will certainly be with him." And then gave him a vision of what he would do after he delivered His people. He said, "When you have brought the people out of Egypt, you shall serve God on this mountain." *(Exodus 3:12)*

Moses thought to himself, *How shall I serve a God I don't know. This is my first encounter with you. All the gods I've ever known have a name, I don't even know your name?"* Approaching this God carefully, and not wanting to ask Him who He was, Moses asked indirectly, "Indeed, when I come to the children of Israel and say to them, 'The God of your fathers has sent me to you' and they say to me, 'What is His name?' what shall I say to them?" *(Exodus 3:13)*

And God said to Moses, "I AM WHO I AM." And He said, "Thus you shall say to the children of Israel, "I AM has sent me to you." He then gave him a detailed strategy to initiate the deliverance. Still not trusting this God, Moses, raised another objection.

He said, "But suppose they will not believe me or listen to my voice; suppose they say, 'The LORD has not appeared to you.'" *(Exodus 4:1)*

Again, ignoring his objection, God decided to demonstrate His unlimited power to Moses. God asked, "What is that in your hand?"

Moses said, "A rod."

And God said, "Cast it on the ground."

So, he cast it on the ground, and it became a serpent; and Moses fled from it.

Then the Lord said to Moses, "Reach out your hand and take it by the tail," (and he reached out his hand and caught it, and it became a rod in his hand), that they may believe that the Lord God of their fathers, the God of Abraham, the God of Isaac, and the God of Jacob, has appeared to you."

Furthermore, the Lord said to him, "Now put your hand in your bosom."

And he put his hand in his bosom, and when he took it out, behold, his hand was leprous, like snow.

And He said, "Put your hand in your bosom again."

So, he put his hand in his bosom again, and drew it out of his bosom, and behold, it was restored like his other flesh.

"Then it will be, if they do not believe you, nor heed the message of the first sign, that they may believe the message of the latter sign." *(Exodus 4:2-8)*

Still reeling from these miraculous demonstrations, Moses thought to himself, *This God has power to materialize snakes and can make me leprous. I'd better pay attention, but I'm still not convinced that I'm the right candidate for the job. I like my tranquil life here where there's no conflict and no demands. But He is powerful, so I have to tread carefully.*

With his thoughts racing, he decided to acknowledge the voice as his Lord, he said, "O my Lord, I am not eloquent, neither before nor since

You have spoken to Your servant; but I am slow of speech and slow of tongue." *(Exodus 4:10)*

God, who is the answer to every objection, responded and asked, "Who has made man's mouth? Or who makes the mute, the deaf, the seeing, or the blind? Have not I, the Lord? Now therefore, go, and I will be with your mouth and teach you what you shall say." *(Exodus 4:12-11)*

Finally expressing his heart to this powerful God, Moses came to the point and said, "O my Lord, please send by the hand of whomever else you may send." *(Exodus 4:13)*

With His anger kindling against Moses' objections, God made it clear that he was His choice and would therefore supply everything he needed to fulfill the task. He said, "Is not Aaron the Levite your brother? I know that he can speak well. And look, he is also coming out to meet you. When he sees you, he will be glad in his heart. Now you shall speak to him and put the words in his mouth. And I will be with your mouth and with his mouth, I will teach you what you shall do. So, he shall be your spokesman to the people. And he himself shall be as a mouth for you, and you shall be to him as God. And you shall take this rod in your hand, with which you shall do the signs." *(Exodus 4:14-17)*

It's at this point, that Moses conceded. There were no further objections. Even though he was still reluctant to accept the task, he heeded the power and authority of the I AM, and prepared to return to Egypt.

CHAPTER 15
DELIVERANCE, FREEDOM AND PROMISES

With his mind still reeling from the encounter with the I AM, the God of his fathers, Moses gathered the sheep and headed home. Processing what had just occurred, he thought, *Did I just see the burning bush, or did I image it? Am I losing my mind? Did my fathers' God speak to me? Why now, that I'm a useless old man, with nothing to offer. My life has been nothing but ashes. I'm a lowly shepherd. All I'm good for now is taking care of sheep. He surely has a great sense of humor.* He then looked at the staff and recalled the fear that ran through him when it turned into a snake, and thought, *That was real.* He also remembered his shock seeing his hand that had turned leprous, and thought, *That was surely real.*

He rehearsed everything he heard and experienced over and over in his mind. Then looking up to heaven for the first time in almost forty years, he said, "You are real. I don't understand why you're choosing me at this age. I'm weak. I have no strength apart from you. If you are sending me to deliver your people, it will be unmistakably You, because I have nothing to give. I am but a sheep in your hand, to do with as you will."

Arriving home, he shared his burning bush encounter with his wife and father-in-law. Still a reluctant but obedient deliverer, Moses packed up his wife and son and then headed to Egypt. On the way however, the Lord made it clear that anything less than total obedience could cost his life. Awaking one day to find his hands white with leprosy, he and his wife recognized it as one of God's recent signs to him. Moses, paralyzed with fear, did not understand what was wrong. His wife, however, recalling Moses recount of the God of the Israelites covenant of circumcision with His people, immediately knew what had to be done. She said to him, accusingly, "You renounced your heritage and the covenant God made to His people, by not circumcising your son. We obviously cannot go any further until we fully commit."

Moses, contemplating choosing death rather than returning to Egypt, remained silent. Seeing his reluctance, his wife, therefore, took a "sharp stone and cut off the foreskin of her son and cast it at Moses' feet, and said, "Surely you are a husband of blood to me!" *(Exodus 4:24)* Honoring Zipporah's act, God immediately returned Moses' hand to normal flesh.

They continued the journey to Egypt. Knowing that Moses needed encouragement, God spoke to his brother, Aaron, and told him to go and meet him. Recognizing each other from a far off, both brother's, now old men, hurried forward and kissed each other. Aaron shared that their parents were dead, but their sister, Miriam, even though an old woman now, was still enthusiastic and excited to see him.

Moses then shared God's strategy and all His signs as they walked towards Egypt. When they arrived, they met with the elders and Aaron shared all that God had instructed his brother to do. Expecting them to raise similar doubts and objections as he did to God at the burning bush, he was shocked when they didn't. "The people believed and when they heard that the LORD had visited the children of Israel and that He had looked on their affliction, then they bowed their heads and worshiped." *(Exodus 4:31)*

Seeing the elders' readiness to believe in the words of the I AM, all of Moses' objections, questions and concerns disappeared. For the first time, he bowed his head, and worshiped the God of his fathers.

The Lord performed all that He said He would do. And through Moses' leadership, He delivered the children of Israel with powerful, signs and mighty wonders. Such that have never been seen or heard of again. The ashes of his life bloomed into a great deliverer and shepherd of God's people. Just as God told him at the burning bush, He returned to mount Horeb. And there, He worshipped God, and spoke to Him, face to face, as a man would speak to an intimate friend.

The light of each worship experience shone just as bright as it did at their first encounter at

the burning bush. However, as a worshipper of
the I AM, the glow of God's presence remained on
Moses, so much so, that he had to cover his face
because the people couldn't look upon him; it was
like looking into the sun. By no means a perfect
man, God chose him, to not only deliver His
people, but to shepherd them. He trusted him
with His laws, His design of the ark that
contained His presence, the template of His
sanctuary, the outline of worship, and so much
more.

   While he led the Israelites to the promise
land, God did not permit him to enter at that
time. God, however, allowed him to see it from
afar, on Mount Nebo. Then approximately forty-
two generations later, his feet stood upon a high
mountain in the promise land. And, with the
Deliverer of the world, Jesus Christ, who was
"transfigured before them. His face shone like the
sun, and His clothes became as white as the
light. And behold, Moses and Elijah appeared to
them, talking with them."

   After Moses joined the heavenly hosts, his
assistant, Joshua, led the people into the promise

land. Through great victories, the children of Israel finally possessed their lands and became a great nation. However, generational discord of jealously, strife and disobedience among the twelve brothers, re-emerged. Joseph's and Benjamin's descendants however, bonded even more closely and eventually settled in a place called Samaria; a place Jesus chose to announce Himself as the Messiah.

BOOK FOUR

ANOTHER DAUGHTER OF JACOB

CHAPTER 1
THE SAMARITANS

More than forty generations after the Israelites exodus from Egypt, Joseph's, Benjamin's and Sychar's descendants were more deeply bonded than ever. Over time, their families had blended through marriage, so much so that Sychar's descendants shared in Joseph's and Benjamin's inheritance. Conversely, seeds of dislike, discord and distrust between their descendants and their ten brothers' descendants, had also deepened.

After fighting for the right to possess their promised lands, Joseph, Benjamin and Sychar's descendants gravitated to the parcel of land they believed Jacob had purchased. Naming their territory Samaria, many settled in that location and eventually became known as Samaritans.

They were a proud people who acknowledged Jacob [Israel] as their forefather. Through tribal conflicts and mutual dislike, they separated from Jacob's older sons' descendants who eventually became known as the Jews. While they shared the same patriarch, inherent discord between the Samaritans and the Jews, passed through the generations. And though they lived side by side, there was an emotional gulf between them, to the extent that they did not acknowledge or speak to each other.

Such was the relationship between the Samaritans and the Jews when Jesus, the Christ, the Messiah, boldly decided to go through Samaria. "He came to a city of Samaria which is called Sychar, near the plot of ground that Jacob gave to his son Joseph. Now Jacob's well was there. Jesus therefore, being wearied from His journey, sat by the well. It was about the sixth hour." *(John 4:5-6)*

CHAPTER 2
THE BAD SAMARITAN

As Jesus rested by the well, Dinah, a Samaritan woman, descendant of Sychar, left her house to get water. Looking left and right before stepping out, she saw that the path was clear and quickly began moving forward. She was singularly focused: walk to the well, get water, and return home without anyone seeing her. Such was her daily routine. Knowing that the other women in the city were not out in the middle of the day, and the men were occupied with their businesses, she hurriedly stepped onto the path that led to the well. With her head covered and bowed low, she hurried, wishing she was invisible.

With her fortieth birthday approaching, she began reflecting on her life and questioned the purpose of living. She had learned from her older sisters that her mother took her last breath as she took her first. Disappointed and distraught at his wife's death and the birth of his seventh daughter, her father named her Dinah, saying, "her life has caused controversy."

Wanting a mother for his seven daughters, her father remarried ~ four times. Two wives died and the other two disappeared. Her father, who struggled to provide for his family, eventually died. Having limited choices, the four oldest sisters did what they could to support their younger sisters. From begging, to peddling, and their last recourse, selling their bodies; they did whatever they could to survive. Dinah, therefore, grew up seeing men coming in and out of their home and learned how to fend for herself at an early age.

Having a charismatic and vivacious personality, she was everyone's favorite and stood out from the crowd. Just like her matriarch and namesake, Dinah, Jacob's daughter, she was taller than the average woman of her time, with jet, black hair that tumbled to her waist. Her piercing, black, almond shaped eyes compelled attention and were perfectly set in a heart shaped face. High cheekbones framed her small nose that sat above exquisitely contoured lips.

Although fully covered in traditional attire of the day, the outline of her figure was exquisite in form and shape. Her countenance, however, was her most attractive feature. Her face and eyes shined with kindness, compassion, and friendliness. She knew no strangers and felt comfortable in any setting.

Vowing for a different life, she accepted her first marriage proposal. Unfortunately, the engagement lasted longer than the actual marriage. For reasons she could not understand, her husband gave her a certificate of divorce and she returned to her childhood home.

Not happy with their sister's failed marriage, her older sisters demanded that she provide for herself. She therefore, married the next man who asked. Four failed marriages later, she became the topic of vicious gossip among the women, and an object of lustful curiosity among the men.

Gaining the reputation of a woman who knew how to get a man, but not keep one, she was scorned and avoided by the women in the village. Men, however, sought her out as a play object, until she met her current husband-to-be, Ben-Oni, [meaning, son of my sorrow].

Ben-Oni, who was twenty years her senior was not her husband. Watching her grow up in the village and knowing her desperate need for a home and stability, he expressed a fatherly interest. Therefore, when he asked if she would be willing to live with him as his companion, she said, "yes." Being a lonely widower and childless, he had enough to provide for her and she longed for stability. Days after she moved in, however, he expressed more than a fatherly interest and demanded his right for what he had purchased. Deceived, disappointed, distraught, alone and desperate, she yielded to his desires. Their living arrangement, however, became the talk of the city. She was ostracized by everyone in the city, including her own family, and became even more of a public disgrace.

CHAPTER 3

THE RECURRING DREAM

Deep in thought, familiar waves of isolation, worthlessness and despair engulfed her soul, she looked up and said, "God of my fathers, if you really exist, I need to know you. If not, my life is a waste, a failure, not even worth the dirt to be disrupted to dig my grave."

She also reflected on the dream she had earlier in the week, in which *she had accidently broken off a small twig from a dry, dead bush. Picking it up from the ground, it crumbled in her hand turning to ashes. Feeling despondent, she threw the ashes in the air. It floated upward and disappeared into the clouds. Then as if returning from nowhere, the ashes floated down and rested on the dead bush. The bush then began growing and kept on growing until it became a gigantic, blooming tree, loaded with different kinds of low hanging fruit.*

Sensing an unseen presence following the dream, she had said, "I am a grain of ash, useful only to be crushed under the feet. You are the God of Jacob. You can do anything. Here I am. I give You my life; do with me whatever you will."

Such were her reflections as she approached the well. She was, therefore, startled when a voice said to her, "Give Me a drink." *(John 4:7)*

Lifting her downcast head, and staring at Him in stunned silence, she was shocked to see someone at the well at that hour. However, even more astonishing was that the person spoke to her, as no one else was around. Recognizing that he was a stranger, and judging from his wardrobe, she assumed that he was a Jewish Rabbi. She replied somewhat dazed, "How is it that You, being a Jew, ask a drink from me, a Samaritan woman?" *(John 4:9)*

Jesus answered and said to her, "If you knew the gift of God, and who it is who says to you 'Give Me a drink' you would have asked Him, and He would have given you living water." *(John 4:10)*

Thinking that he was like the other men in her life, always taking, and making empty promises, she looked at him suspiciously, then looked around him. Seeing that he had nothing to hold water or give water, she sarcastically, asked, "Sir, you have nothing to draw with and the well is deep. Where then do You get that living water?" *He must think I'm stupid or he believes he's God and can do anything. I'll let him know that I'm no fool,* she thought to herself. Then she added aloud, "Are you greater than our father Jacob, who gave us the well and drank from it himself, as well as his sons and his livestock?" *(John 4:11-12)*

Addressing her need and ignoring her question, Jesus answered and said to her, "Whoever drinks of this water will thirst again, but whoever drinks of the water that I shall give him will never thirst. But the water that I shall give him will become in him a fountain of water springing up into everlasting life." *(John 4:14)*

Now even more suspicious than before, and still believing that he had nothing to offer, as the other men she had encountered, she challenged Him and said, "Sir, give me this water, that I may not thirst, nor come here to draw." *(John 4:15)*

Already knowing everything about her, Jesus said, "Go, call your husband, and come here." *(John 4:16)*

Believing that the stranger was probing into her private life for ulterior motives, she dryly answered, "I have no husband." *(John 4:17)*

Jesus said to her, "You have well said, 'I have no husband' for you have had five husbands, and the one whom you now have is not your husband; in that you spoke truly." *(John 4:17-18)*

Discerning that there was something different about this man, her eyes flashed with interest. She replied, "Sir, I perceive that You are a prophet." Wanting to probe into His religious knowledge and divert the conversation away from her life, she commented, "Our fathers worshiped on this mountain, and you Jews say that in Jerusalem is the place where one ought to worship." *(John 4:20)*

Jesus relied, "Woman, believe Me, the hour is coming when you will neither on this mountain nor in Jerusalem, worship the Father. You worship what you do not know; we know what we worship, for salvation is of the Jews. But the hour is coming, and now is, when the true worshipers will worship the Father in spirit and in truth; for the Father is seeking such to worship Him. God is Spirit, and those who worship Him must worship in spirit and truth." *(John 4:21-24)*

Her heart raced with hope. *He already knows everything about me and he's still talking to me. Not only is He talking to me, but He's telling me things about God, referring to Him as Father. I've never heard anyone talk like this before. Who is He? I wonder what he really knows about the Messiah. I'll put him to the test,* she thought to herself.

She said, "I know that Messiah is coming (who is called the Christ). When He comes, He will tell us all things." *(John 4:25)*

Jesus proclaimed, "I who speak to you am He." *(John 4:26)*

Silence invaded her soul as she processed what she just heard. Her mind began racing and she thought, *Did he just say that He was the Messiah? I wanted to know what He knew about the Messiah, but He said He was the Messiah? He did tell me about my husbands and current living relationship. If He knew that, then everything else He said must be true.*

With her heart overflowing with seeds of new life, she stared at him in awe. Seeing a group of men approaching, she decided to flee. Without another word, she left her water pitcher that was heavy and burdensome, at his feet, and ran back to the city to share her extraordinary experience.

CHAPTER 4

REDEMPTION – THE FIRST

FEMALE EVANGELIST

Dinah couldn't wait to share her news with anyone who would listen. She was amazed that the man she met at the well spoke to her, an outcast, a nobody, a dry, broken twig. No longer ashamed or intimidated, she ran into the public square where she knew the men of the town gathered. Standing in the middle of the square, she stood and boldly announced, "Come, see a Man who told me all things that I ever did. Could this be the Christ?" *(John 4:29)*

The men immediately began whispering among themselves. Some were shocked and others curious, but all were interested. She then went up to each one and repeated what she said. The hope in her eyes, the conviction in her voice and the transformation in her countenance convinced them that whoever this man was, they wanted to meet him.

Following her, they reached the well and saw several Jewish men talking. There was one, however, whose voice stood out from them all. He had just said to his disciples, "Lift up your eyes and look at the fields, for they are already white for harvest!" And as they lifted their eyes, they saw a large crowd of men approaching, with a woman in their midst. *(John 4:35)*

Upon seeing them approaching, Jesus stepped forward and stood in front of Dinah. Locking gaze with her, He warmly welcomed her back. The men stared in awe, because the woman had told them that, "He told me all the things that I ever did." *(John 4:29)* Yet, there He was, a Jewish Rabbi, speaking kindly to the one they considered to be the lowest of the low.

Turning to the men, he greeted them with His captivating smile and friendly voice. They were even more stunned, knowing that if He knew everything she ever did, He also knew everything they ever did. And yet, this Rabbi, greeted them with warmth, kindness, compassion and love. No

Jew had ever done that, especially not a Jewish Rabbi. Then "many of the Samaritans of that city believed in Him because of the word of the woman who testified, "He told me all that I ever did." *(John 4:39)*

They "urged Him to stay with them; and He stayed there two days." *(John 4:40)* Word quickly spread throughout the city about this unusual teacher. And later that day, the entire city [women and children] came out to meet Him.

For the next two days, they listened transfixed on His every word. And beginning from before the creation of the world, through Abraham, Isaac, and Jacob, through their forefathers, Joseph and Benjamin, through David, all the kings and prophets; He taught them as One who not only knew history, but as One telling His story.

His words and eyes penetrated their souls. He spoke of his Father's love for them, and His love for them. He told them of His Father's Kingdom and what He had prepared for them. Every word overflowed their hearts with hope, new life and love.

And many believed because of His own word. They then said to the woman, "Now we believe, not because of what you said, for we ourselves have heard Him and we know that this is indeed the Christ, the Savior of the world." *(John 4:41-42)*

Samaria and Sychar were never the same. Dinah and all those who heard Him were forever changed. Many followed when He left the city, including Dinah. Choosing not to return to her dwelling, she left everything, including her past and followed the stranger who satisfied her thirst with living water.

Months later, "a certain lawyer stood up and tested Him, [Jesus], by asking, 'Who is my neighbor?'" *(Luke 10:29)*

Looking directly at Dinah, whom He had renamed "EveMarie," and gazing lovingly at his other Samaritan followers, Jesus shared the story about a certain Samaritan. Knowing the implications of the story and what He was about to say to this lawyer and the Jewish crowd, He boldly told them to follow the example of the Samaritan. *(Luke 10-30-37)*

EveMarie followed her Messiah wherever He went. She was at the Cross and the Upper Room. Courageously and confidently sharing her encounter with the man at the well, she always began with, "Let me tell you about a man who told me everything I ever did. He spoke to me when no one else would. He loved and accepted me when others crushed me under their feet like dry leaves. He exchanged my stagnated, filthy water for living water that restores my soul. Surely, He is the Christ, the Son of the Living God, our Messiah."

Her story became well known throughout the region and many came to believe in Him. This descendant of Jacob's daughter, Dinah, a dead twig, arising from the ashes of another dry, broken twig, became the first female evangelist, spreading the exciting news of the Messiah, Jesus Christ.

The End

ABOUT THE AUTHOR

*"...But God has chosen the foolish things of the
world, to put to shame the wise and God has
chosen the weak things of the world to put to
shame the things which are mighty; and the base
things of the world and the things which are
despised God has chosen,
and the things which are not, to bring to nothing
the things that are, that no flesh should glory
in His presence."*
1Corinthians 1:27-29

I have the words "that's me," written next to the above text in my bible. I was born and raised on a small island in the Caribbean until age 14 when I joined my mother in Connecticut. What a culture shock! I'm still recovering from winter.

My journey since then has led me to live in several states on the East Coast, West Coast and now the Midwest. I have a B.S. in Sociology, MS in Human Resources and Business, plenty of real time, hands-on experience with life, and most importantly, an intimate relationship with my Lord, Jesus Christ. I enjoy writing, reading, gardening, travelling and spending time with family and friends.

You've heard some of my story. I would love to hear yours. You can reach me at, www.a2zredemption.com

BOOKS BY W. A. VEGA

The thrilling, Christian <u>A-Z Redemption</u> series:

Extraordinary Gifts (Volume 1)

A Place Called Hell-O (Volume 2)

Incredible Inheritance (Volume 3)

The Surrogate's Sons (Volume 4)

www.A2ZRedemption.com

The Thought Provoking <u>Beyond Religion</u> series:

The Adventures of A. Soul, Volume 1

400 Kingdom of Heaven Perspectives, Volume 2

Through Weak Eyes, Volume 3

Indescribable, Volume 4

She has also authored:

Mi Cara, Letters From Heaven